By Choice or By Chance?

*Tracking the Values
  in Massachusetts' Public Spending*

PIONEER PAPER NO. 6

By Choice or By Chance?

*Tracking the Values
in Massachusetts' Public Spending*

Herman B. Leonard

With a Foreword by
David Warsh

Published by

Pioneer Institute for Public Policy Research
Boston, Massachusetts
1992

Pioneer Institute is an independent, nonprofit research organization funded by individuals, corporations, and foundations. Pioneer Papers and Dialogues are published for educational purposes, to assist policymakers, and to broaden public understanding of critical social and economic issues. Views expressed in the Institute's publications are those of the authors and not necessarily those of the Pioneer staff, advisors, or directors, nor should they be construed as an attempt to influence any election or legislative action.

Cover Art: Lafayette Graphics, Worcester, Massachusetts
Desktop Publishing: Kathryn Ciffolillo
Printing: Davis Press, Worcester, Massachusetts

Library of Congress Cataloging-in-Publication Data

Leonard, Herman B.
    By choice or by chance? : tracking the values in Massachusetts'
public spending / Herman B. Leonard.
        p.   cm. — (Pioneer paper series ; no. 6)
    "January 1992."
    ISBN 0-929930-08-8 : $10.00
    1. Government spending policy—Massachusetts—Econometric models.
2. Government spending policy—United States—States—Econometric
models. 3. Expenditures, Public—Econometric models. I. Title.
II. Series.
HJ7595.L46   1992
336.3'9'09744—dc20   92-7665
                                                                CIP

Pioneer Institute
for Public Policy Research

Pioneer Institute is a public policy research organization that specializes in the support, distribution, and promotion of scholarly research on Massachusetts public policy issues. Its main program—the Pioneer Paper series—consists of research projects commissioned from area scholars. The Institute publishes these papers and communicates the research results to decision makers in government and opinion leaders in business, academia, and the media. Pioneer Institute is supported by corporate, foundation, and individual contributions and qualifies under IRS rules for 501 (c)(3) tax-exempt status.

Pioneer Institute recognizes the generous support of its members. It is only with your support—financial and otherwise—that Pioneer can continue to publish studies and sponsor educational forums and discussions.

Thank you.

To Whitney and Dana

CONTENTS

FOREWORD   xvii
David Warsh

ACKNOWLEDGMENTS   xxiii

CHAPTER ONE: Divided We Spend   1

Income Growth from 1979 to 1989   1
Proposition 2½   3
The Reduction in Federal Support   4
The Shift in Public Spending Patterns   4
The Shift in Spending Priorities   6
Spending Choices   8
Previous Comparative Studies of State Spending   9
The Approach   11
Components   14
Organization of the Study   16

CHAPTER TWO: Public Education   18

Public Elementary and Secondary Education   20
Forming the Benchmark   20
The Dispersion of Priorities   20
Pattern of Massachusetts' Relative Priority over Time   22
Understanding the Difference between Massachusetts
and the National Average   23
Understanding the Change in Massachusetts' Elementary
and Secondary Education Spending, 1979–1989   25
Public Higher Education   26
Forming the Benchmark   26
Pattern of Massachusetts' Relative Priority over Time   27
The Dispersion of Priorities   28

Understanding the Difference between Massachusetts
and the National Average 28
Understanding the Change in Massachusetts' Higher
Education Spending, 1979-1989 31
Commentary 32

CHAPTER THREE: Human Services 35

Direct Assistance 36
Forming the Benchmark 37
Pattern of Massachusetts' Relative Priority over Time 38
The Dispersion of Priorities 39
Understanding the Difference between Massachusetts
and the National Average 39
Understanding the Change in Massachusetts' Direct
Assistance Spending, 1979-1989 42
Health and Hospitals 43
Forming the Benchmark 44
Pattern of Massachusetts' Relative Priority over Time 45
The Dispersion of Priorities 46
Understanding the Difference between Massachusetts
and the National Average 46
Understanding the Change in Massachusetts' Health and
Hospitals Spending, 1979-1989 47
Commentary 48

CHAPTER FOUR: Highways 50

Forming the Benchmark for Highways 50
Highway Operating Expenditures 51
Pattern of Massachusetts' Relative Priority over Time 52
The Dispersion of Priorities 53
Understanding the Difference between Massachusetts
and the National Average 53

Understanding the Change in Massachusetts' Highway
    Spending, 1979–1989   55
Total Highway Spending (including capital)   56
Pattern of Massachusetts' Relative Priority over Time   57
The Dispersion of Priorities   58
Understanding the Difference between Massachusetts
    and the National Average   58
Understanding the Change in Massachusetts' Highway
    Spending, 1979–1989   58
Commentary   61

CHAPTER FIVE: Public Safety and Corrections   63

Forming the Benchmarks for Public Safety
    and Corrections   63
Public Safety (excluding Corrections)   64
Pattern of Massachusetts' Relative Priority over Time   64
Understanding the Change in Massachusetts' Public
    Safety Spending, 1979–1989   65
Understanding the Difference between Massachusetts
    and the National Average   67
The Dispersion of Priorities   67
Corrections   67
Understanding the Difference between Massachusetts
    and the National Average   70
Pattern of Massachusetts' Relative Priority over Time   71
The Dispersion of Priorities   72
Understanding the Change in Massachusetts' Corrections
    Spending, 1979–1989   73
Commentary   74

CHAPTER SIX: Total General Expenditures   76

Forming the Benchmark   77
Pattern of Massachusetts' Relative Priority over Time   78

The Dispersion of Priorities 79
Understanding the Difference between Massachusetts
    and the National Average 81
Understanding the Change in Massachusetts'
    Spending, 1979–1989 82
Commentary 84

**CHAPTER SEVEN: Massachusetts' Spending Priorities:
By Choice or By Chance?** 85

Why did Massachusetts' Value Choices Change? 88
What are Massachusetts' Value Choices Now? 90
Where from Here? 94

APPENDIX A: Methods and Approach 97

A New Approach 100
Constructing the Right Comparison 102
Sensitivity of the Estimates 118
Form of the Estimating Equations 119
Reporting the Results 120
Interpretation of Statistical Results 125
Expenditure Data Sources 127

APPENDIX B: Data Sources and Adjustments 129

Spending Areas Used in Study 130
Adjustments to Expenditure Data 134
Sources of Demographic and Characteristic Data 138
Sources of Political Culture Data 143

APPENDIX C: Benchmark Estimating Equations 163

LIST OF FIGURES AND TABLES

Figure 1-1: Percent Change in Real Per Capita Income,   3
1979-1989

Figure 1-2: Percent Change in State Share of Spending
(before transfers), 1979-1989   7

Figure 2-1: Elementary and Secondary OperatingExpenditures
per Pupil, Difference from Benchmark, 1979   21

Figure 2-2: Elementary and Secondary Education Operating
Expenditures per Pupil (Massachusetts)   23

Table 2-1: Reconciliation of National Average to Massachusetts
Spending, Public Elementary and Secondary Education
Operating Spending per Enrolled Student, 1989   24

Table 2-2: Analysis of 1979-1989 Change in Real Massachusetts
Spending, Public Elementary and Secondary Education
Operating Spending per Enrolled Student   25

Figure 2-3: Higher Education Operating Expenditures per
Pupil (Massachusetts)   27

Figure 2-4: Higher Education Operating Expenditures per
Pupil, Difference from Benchmark, 1989   29

Table 2-3: Reconciliation of National Average to Massachusetts
Spending, Public Higher Education Operating Spending per
Enrolled Student, 1989   30

Table 2-4: Decomposition of 1979-1989 Change in Real
Massachusetts Spending, Public Higher Education Operating
Spending per Enrolled Student   32

Figure 3-1: Net Direct Assistance per Poor Person
(Massachusetts)   38

Figure 3-2: Direct Assistance per Poor Person (Net of Federal
Reimbursement), Difference from Benchmark, 1979
and 1989   40

Table 3-1: Reconciliation of National Average to Massachusetts Spending, Direct Assistance Net State Spending per Poor Person, 1989   42

Table 3-2: Analysis of 1979–1989 Change in Real Massachusetts Spending, Direct Assistance Net State Spending per Poor Person   43

Figure 3-3: Net Health and Hospital Expenditures per Capita (Massachusetts)   45

Figure 3-4: Net Health and Hospital Expenditures per Capita, Difference from Benchmark, 1989   46

Table 3-3: Reconciliation of National Average to Massachusetts Spending, Health and Hospitals Net State Spending per Capita, 1989   47

Table 3-4: Analysis of 1979–1989 Change in Real Massachusetts Spending, Health and Hospitals Net State Spending per Capita   48

Figure 4-1: Highway Operating Expenditures per Vehicle (Massachusetts)   52

Figure 4-2: Highway Operating Expenditures per Vehicle, Difference from Benchmark, 1989   54

Table 4-1: Reconciliation of National Average to Massachusetts Spending, Highway Operating Spending per Motor Vehicle, 1989   55

Table 4-2: Analysis of 1979–1989 Change in Real Massachusetts Spending, Highway Operating Spending per Motor Vehicle   56

Figure 4-3: Total Highway Expenditures per Vehicle (Massachusetts)   57

Figure 4-4: Total Highway Expenditures per Vehicle, Difference from Benchmark, 1989   59

Table 4-3: Reconciliation of National Average to Massachusetts Spending, Total Highway Spending per Motor Vehicle, 1989   60

Table 4-4: Analysis of 1979–1989 Change in Real Massachusetts
Spending, Total Highway Spending per Motor Vehicle   61
Figure 5-1: Public Safety Expenditures per Capita
(Massachusetts)   65
Table 5-1: Analysis of 1979–1989 Change in Real Massachusetts
Spending, Public Safety Spending per Capita   66
Table 5-2: Reconciliation of National Average to Massachusetts
Spending, Public Safety Spending (excluding Corrections)
per Capita, 1989   68
Figure 5-2: Public Safety Expenditures per Capita, Difference
from Benchmark, 1989   69
Table 5-3: Reconciliation of National Average to Massachusetts
Spending, Corrections Spending per Capita, 1989   70
Figure 5-3: Correction Expenditures per Capita
(Massachusetts)   71
Figure 5-4: Correction Expenditures per Capita, Difference
from Benchmark, 1989   72
Table 5-4: Analysis of 1979–1989 Change in Real Massachusetts
Spending, Corrections Spending per Capita   73
Figure 6-1: Net General Expenditures per Capita
(Massachusetts)   78
Figure 6-2: Net General Expenditures per Capita, Difference
from Benchmark, 1989   80
Table 6-1: Reconciliation of National Average to Massachusetts
Spending, General Expenditures Net of Federal
Reimbursements per Capita, 1989   82
Table 6-2: Decomposition of 1979–1989 Change in Real
Massachusetts Spending, General Expenditures Net of
Federal Reimbursements per Capita   83
Table 7-1: Changes in Differences between Actual and Benchmark
Spending, Massachusetts, 1979–1989   87
Table 7-2: Summary of Differences between Actual and
Benchmark Spending, Massachusetts, 1989   90

Table 7-3: Summary of Aggregate Budget Differences between
    Actual and Benchmark Spending, Massachusetts, 1989   93
Figure A-1: Nominal Elementary and Secondary Education
    Expenditures per Capita, 1989   98
Table A-1: Commonly Used Explanatory Variables   115
Table A-2: Political Culture Variables   117
Table B-1: Index to Data Series, Variable Description   147
Table B-2: Sample Statistics on Data Series (1989)   149
Table B-3: Sample Statistics on Data Series (1988)   150
Table B-4: Sample Statistics on Data Series (1987)   151
Table B-5: Sample Statistics on Data Series (1986)   152
Table B-6: Sample Statistics on Data Series (1985)   153
Table B-7: Sample Statistics on Data Series (1984)   154
Table B-8: Sample Statistics on Data Series (1983)   155
Table B-9: Sample Statistics on Data Series (1982)   156
Table B-10: Sample Statistics on Data Series (1981)   157
Table B-11: Sample Statistics on Data Series (1980)   158
Table B-12: Sample Statistics on Data Series (1979)   159
Table B-13: Massachusetts Adjusted Annual
    Expenditures   160
Table B-14: Massachusetts Demographic and Political
    Characteristics   161
Table C-1: Benchmark Regression Coefficient Estimates   164

FOREWORD

Businessmen seeking to do business in Poland have a standard joke about Warsaw: Paris prices and Albanian service levels. This verbal formula captures nicely the kind of variance whose important mysteries are at the heart of this little book.

It has been nearly 20 years since Massachusetts was first convulsed by the movement that we have come to know as the "tax revolt." That was 1974, and a new governor named Michael S. Dukakis came to power on the strength of his promise not to raise taxes. Since then, public antipathy to the more expansive tendencies of government has broadened out, deepened, and spread around the world as far as Poland and Albania. Sentiment has even turned back on itself occasionally, and swept away many leaders who failed to read its course, including Margaret Thatcher, Mikhail Gorbachev and Michael Dukakis.

Throughout, public debate has been focused by a closely related series of questions having to do with budgets. What fraction of national income do citizens wish to spend on governments altogether? For what purposes should it be spent? How best to organize spending? How do the decisions that are made about these questions feed back into the economic life of communities? How do they produce the enormous variations in the standard of living that are exemplified by our mental images of Paris, Warsaw and Tirana?

To questions like these, this study by Herman "Dutch" Leonard, professor of public finance at the John F. Kennedy School of Government at Harvard University, promises to make a long-lasting contribution. *By Choice or By Chance?* affords a methodology that permits citizens and their representatives to see their choices clearly, for what they are. It will facilitate comparisons among the states over time—comparisons that now take place almost entirely in the mind's eye, or worse, with loaded numbers.

Comparing spending by category among the states of America is nothing new. Citizens are accustomed to hearing politicians and activists claim that Massachusetts has the highest per capita This or lowest per capita That. They are equally accustomed to hearing these assertions challenged for their failure to reflect one or another special aspect of the situation in question. My favorite is the assertion that, because Massachusetts spends less on public higher education than most other states, it is somehow failing to turn out an educated work force!

Now it is well known that the cost of living varies substantially from place to place. A salary of $30,000 goes pretty far in Michigan, where prices are low; it doesn't serve nearly as well in Massachusetts. The costs of rendering government services thus vary from place to place, as do all the other costs of living.

Likewise, some of the most elemental *requirements* for government service vary from place to place, because the climate and the population mix differ. Florida, Arizona and Massachusetts have somewhat older populations and thus higher Medicaid bills. West Virginia and Kentucky have a lot of rural poverty and proportionately greater welfare costs. New York City has an extensive—and expensive—rail infrastructure.

Finally, everybody recognizes that political cultures differ from state to state and from year to year—and that these cultures deeply inform spending decisions. For more than a century, Massachusetts and Wisconsin have prided themselves on being home to progressive ideals. Minnesota has become synonymous with clean and innovative government. New Hampshire has a flinty political culture of which its citizens are proud. Southern states have more poverty and a different set of attitudes for dealing with it. These bred-in-the-bone political traits make a measurable difference in what each state spends on a given task of government.

What Professor Leonard has done is to take some—perhaps most—of the funny business out of these comparisons, by systematically adjusting for these variations. Readers who turn quickly to appendix A will see the careful methodology that he has devised to separate these various underlying fiscal "circumstances," as he calls them, from the "choices" that voters make from place to place. (Political culture being very much a matter of "choice," Leonard nevertheless has to estimate the extent to which these factors influence spending levels, lest differences be attributed to "circumstances," such as demographic factors.) Readers who then turn to appendix B will discern the scrupulous standards Leonard has observed in assembling his database, most of it from the Bureau of the Census annual survey of government finances.

Leonard's procedure is analogous in many ways to the manipulations you would perform in your head if you were thinking of moving to some far state and were comparing house prices, here and there. First you would factor out the sheer geographic variations in the cost of a certain sort of house, by using a price index; then you might factor out the extent to which purely local conditions, such as the shape and size of the city, affected the price of your home. What remained would be a benchmark cost of housing, against which to choose just how much house to buy this time—a little more or a little less, depending on your personal values.

What emerges from Leonard's efforts are a series of benchmarks for talking with real confidence about state spending patterns—not just their levels, but changing trends over time. Already some startling conclusions have jumped out. For example, it was the generally accepted view in policy circles before the Leonard study that spending on primary and secondary education in Massachusetts had remained high throughout the 1980s, despite the shock to local aid engendered by the passage of Proposition 2½. The state had picked up the difference, it was said.

But Leonard shows that the tumultuous fiscal shifts of the 1980s actually cloaked a dramatic change in priorities—whether accidental or intentional, it is hard to say. In 1979, on the eve of its boom, Massachusetts' spending on public elementary and secondary education was the highest in the nation, more than $900 per pupil greater than the state's benchmark. But by 1989, even though spending on education had steadily climbed in dollar terms, it hadn't climbed fast enough to keep pace: the state had moved to the middle of the national distribution, falling behind 20 other states.

Was this relative neglect of education deliberate? Was it compatible with the economic strategy of a state determined to make its future in the growth of high value-added industries, as the recent study *The Competitive Advantage of Massachusetts* by Michael Porter suggests? Probably not. Professor Leonard's robust findings, which were reported to the public in preliminary form in the autumn of 1991, almost certainly played a key role in Governor William Weld's decision to commit an extra $200 million to K-12 education in his fiscal 1993 budget.

Indeed, the rest of the picture that emerges from Leonard's survey is about what you'd expect from the tenor of the recent discussion. Liberal Massachusetts did indeed spend a good deal more during the 1980s on direct assistance to the poor (a 19 percent increase from its benchmark rate) and health and hospitals (a 32 percent increase above the trend). The state spent a little less than its habit on highways and public safety. And even while it was shorting its allocation to elementary and high schools, Massachusetts upped its (chronically small) ante for higher education a little, surpassing seven states in the level of its spending.

It ought to be noted firmly that there is nothing intrinsically political about this study. It is quite possible to argue that there was nothing accidental about the choices Massachusetts made during the 1980s. Indeed, former Governor Dukakis—now Professor Dukakis—was one of 19 public policy experts who participated in the careful going-over this study received on technical grounds before its publication. He notes that spending on highways fell relatively because the Dukakis and Sargent Administrations elected "to stop spending billions on massive, destructive and unworkable urban expressways" and focused instead on building up public transportation. Similarly, he says, the relative decrease in spending on education statewide may have happened, but it camouflaged a dramatic increase in spending on education in older urban communities—also a matter of deliberate choice, he says. Fair enough—but it always helps to have a clear picture of the choices as they are being made.

It is fitting that this work should have been done by someone so intimately involved in his times as Herman Leonard. (They call him "Dutch" because his middle name is Beukema, his grandfather the latest of a long line of Holland Dutch immigrants to Michigan—and a nationally recognized scholar in his own day.) A 1974 graduate of Harvard College, Leonard received his Ph.D. in 1979, having been taught the intricacies of modern public finance by, among others, Martin Feldstein. Feldstein is in certain ways the avatar of the public policy analyst in the age of Ronald Reagan and George Bush. Professor Leonard's 1986 book about off-budget outlays, *Checks Unbalanced: The Quiet Side of Public Spending,* shows the author to be among the most imaginative of those of his generation who have sought to see clearly the enormous fiscal engine of government. But it was Harvard's legendary Richard Musgrave, representative of an older, more activist Harvard tradition, who really fired Leonard with enthusiasm for the analyst's task. And evidence that these careful, often dry, always intricate statistical studies have a very concrete and significant contribution to make to government can be found on nearly every page.

Leonard promises to keep current his database; statistics for the key year of 1990 will be available by mid-1992, he says. A widening circle of analysts from among the states can be expected to employ the methodology of this pioneering study. And soon, a new generation of government performance measures will begin to make their appearance, enabling us to begin to understand the efficiency with which basic public services like education, public safety and health care are provided from state to state. Then, our comparisons of the role of governments state-by-state will begin to have some real content.

Finally, a word ought to be said about the late Warren Brookes. Among journalists, Warren virtually invented the style of argument from data that Dutch Leonard has now taken to a permanently higher plane. How he would have loved reading this volume!

DAVID WARSH

The Boston Globe

ACKNOWLEDGMENTS

This study could not have been completed but for the help of many, to all of whom I am deeply grateful.

I had the benefit of excellent research assistance. Sydney Rubin helped in the initial phases of building the database. Paul Shadle worked on and supervised the construction of the databank, oversaw the quality assurance effort involved, and provided able research assistance throughout the analysis of the data and the writing of the study. Monica Friar conducted and directed the process of adjusting the data for input cost differences and inflation, carried out the bulk of the estimation of cost models, and made many useful suggestions about how best to compute the necessary adjustments in the data and about approaches to carrying out the analysis and to presenting the results. Susan Parker Viglianti conducted the search for and analysis of the political culture variables, carried out much of the early research on their impacts, and made many helpful proposals about how the study could be improved. Paul, Monica and Susan also made many helpful editorial suggestions about the manuscript. They also contributed to creating a spirit of teamwork and cooperation that made the project more pleasant for all of us. Mary Naus helped to keep us organized, provided general encouragement, and tolerated periodic incursions into her workspace with her remarkable charm, equanimity, and good humor.

I am also grateful to Helen Ladd and Katharine Bradbury, each of whom read a complete first draft and provided detailed technical and editorial suggestions as well as pointing out a number of corrections in interpretation and analysis of the data and results. This report has been greatly improved as a result of their assistance.

Susan Bender edited the report with patience and persistence, streamlining the language, cutting away at inessential diversions from the main thread of the argument, and turning up the volume of the central themes. The debt owed to her by all readers can be assessed by a careful comparison of these acknowledgments—which she did not edit—with the remainder of this report.

The data collection, research, and analysis on which this study is based, and the writing of this report, were supported by the Pioneer Institute of Boston, Massachusetts. Various members of the Pioneer staff helped to suggest research questions and approaches and pointed insistently to the nature of the audience that needed to be addressed. I am especially indebted to Lovett Peters, Ginny Straus, and Charles Baker, Jr., each of whom pointed to important intellectual challenges and provided continuing energy. They recognized that the independence of the conduct, content, and findings of the study were an essential ingredient to whatever impact the results might have.

I also appreciate the many helpful comments I received from the panel of peer reviewers organized by the Pioneer Institute, which included:

Hadley Arkes	Laurence Moss
Brigitte Berger	Harold Petersen
Karl Case	Simon Rottenberg
Paul Cronin	John Rowe
William M. Crozier, Jr.	Richard Schmalensee
Michael Dukakis	Robert Tannenwald
Barbara Dyer	Susanne Tompkins
Nathan Glazer	Raymond Torto
Steven Gold	

As always, my largest debt is to my family. Each member was patient in her own special way.

CHAPTER ONE

Divided We Spend

Many explanations have been offered of how the Commonwealth of Massachusetts came to be mired in an unprecedented fiscal crisis. More are probably needed. Many features of the Massachusetts fiscal landscape changed markedly during the 1980s, some more than once, and in many different directions. This study highlights major shifts in public services spending so that implicit and explicit fiscal choices made over the past decade may be examined in a clearer light.

Four central phenomena go far toward explaining what happened to spending on public services in Massachusetts over the decade. The first was the growth of personal income. The second was Proposition 2½. The third was a decline in federal financial support for state and local government-operated programs. Together, these produced the fourth: a substantial shift in the locus of public spending away from local governments and toward the state treasury.

Income Growth from 1979 to 1989

Personal income is the engine that drives spending, both public and private. The average level of disposable income helps predict the nature and level of consumption by individuals, cities, states, countries; when incomes change substantially the results can be profound.

The average level of personal income in Massachusetts changed dramatically from 1979 to 1989. In 1979, per capita income stood at about $14,000 (expressed in real 1989 dollars[1]), $300 less than the national average; 26 states had higher per capita real incomes. By 1989, per capita income in Massachusetts had risen to over $19,000, and only four states had higher incomes. After adjustment for inflation, per capita income in the state rose by 39 percent over the course of a decade. Only New Hampshire, starting from a lower base in 1979 and buoyed by the same regional economic expansion as Massachusetts, experienced more rapid real growth in income. Figure 1-1 shows a chart of the states arranged by their rates of expansion in real income over the 1979–1989 period. Only five states experienced real income growth over 35 percent; four of the five were in New England.

Over the course of a decade, Massachusetts residents' ability to purchase goods and services expanded by about two-fifths. This rate of sustained real income expansion is nearly unprecedented, even viewed against the rapid expansion of the U.S. economy and the economies of many of the states since World War II. Private businesses in the Commonwealth rode the crest of an enormous expansion in local purchasing power combined with a substantial increase in demand worldwide for products that Massachusetts was well positioned to provide.

The result in the public sector was equally impressive. Total revenues received by state and local government units rose by nearly 25 percent in real terms from 1979 to 1989. As in most states, Massachusetts' state tax revenue base relies heavily on a combination of income and sales taxation, and both the income tax base and the sales tax base grew rapidly with the general economic expansion. As

---

1   The word "real," as a modifier of income, costs, or expenditures, will be used to mean "adjusted for inflation" throughout this study. The data are adjusted by an index reflecting the relative cost of living in each state and the changes in cost over time. *In this study, all figures are stated in real terms, reported in constant 1989 dollars, unless explicitly indicated to the contrary.*

a result, public expenditures also expanded rapidly—in spite of a number of tax cuts enacted by the state government in the mid-1980s.

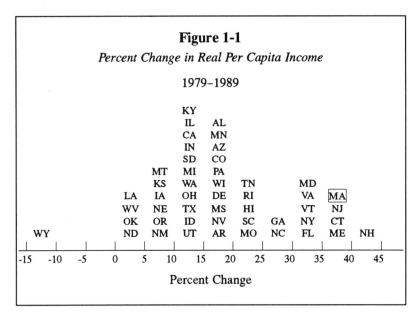

Figure 1-1

Percent Change in Real Per Capita Income

1979–1989

				KY						
				IL	AL					
				CA	MN					
				IN	AZ					
				SD	CO					
			MT	MI	PA					
			KS	WA	WI	TN		MD		
		LA	IA	OH	DE	RI		VA	MA	
		WV	NE	TX	MS	HI		VT	NJ	
		OK	OR	ID	NV	SC	GA	NY	CT	
WY		ND	NM	UT	AR	MO	NC	FL	ME	NH

-15   -10   -5   0   5   10   15   20   25   30   35   40   45

Percent Change

Proposition 2½

Proposition 2½ was approved by voters on November 4, 1980; its major direct impacts were first felt in the 1982 fiscal year. It provided an overall limit on the allowable level and growth of property taxation by communities. It restricted the total property tax levy to 2½ percent of market value, and limited the annual increase on the levy to 2½ percent as well. These limits could be exceeded only by new development or if approved by a popular referendum.

In many communities, existing property taxes exceeded the new limits, and substantial decreases were forced. In others, the general limit was not constraining, but the limit on the rate of increase of the levy resulted in a steady pressure on local budgets. While the override provisions in the law in theory permitted communities to levy higher taxes if they chose, overrides often proved difficult to carry. The advent of Proposition 2½ thus heralded a period in which revenues at the local level would almost certainly decline in inflation-adjusted terms.

The immediate impacts were obvious. Communities around the state faced substantial pressure to reduce local spending, the major components of which are schooling (by far the largest single item) and public safety. Local officials found themselves operating under real fiscal stress. They turned to the state government for relief.

The Reduction in Federal Support

The election of Ronald Reagan in November 1980 created a watershed in the financial relationship between state and local governments, on the one hand, and the federal government, on the other. Two decades of substantial increases in federal support for public programs operated at the state and local level came to an abrupt halt. Nationally, the change would be less dramatic than it was advertised to be: in cost-of-living-adjusted terms, federal support was approximately the same in 1989 as it had been in 1979; the growth in federal support simply ended. Massachusetts, however, had enjoyed greater than average federal assistance—and now felt a greater than average shift. In real terms, federal funding of state and local programs in Massachusetts declined by 24 percent over the decade. The federal share of total Massachusetts spending fell by nearly one-half. The Commonwealth faced a choice between making up the difference out of its own funds or cutting services.

The Shift in Public Spending Patterns

The forces that would shift public spending patterns were in place by the early 1980s. The local tax base, heavily concentrated on property taxes, was (and is) relatively inelastic with respect to economic expansion.[2] Thus, even without Proposition 2½, the local

---

2 Indeed, it is designed to be. One of the principal virtues of the local property tax base is that it is not volatile with respect to economic conditions, so the revenues that can be collected on it are stable. This is thought to help local

tax base would have expanded substantially less than the state government's tax base over the course of the 1980s. With Proposition 2½ in place, that effect was magnified. Local officials faced severe limitations on their capacity to raise local revenues, while the demand for local public services remained strong. Noting the rapid expansion of revenues at the state level, they put pressure on the state government to expand local aid payments to cities and towns. Meanwhile, declining federal contributions pressured the state to increase its own support for programs formerly bankrolled by federal funds.

The state government did substantially expand its local aid payments, spurring a significant change in established patterns of financing public expenditures. While the overall combined real self-financed spending of state and local governments in Massachusetts grew by about 40 percent over the decade (somewhat below the average of about 50 percent for all 50 states), spending by local governments financed out of their own revenues *declined* by 7 percent. Local governments experienced a larger drop in self-financed expenditures in only one other state.

By contrast, state-financed expenditures expanded substantially. When state aid to local governments is included as a state expenditure, real state spending in Massachusetts increased by 88 percent (the average nationwide was less than 50 percent); excluding such state aid, the remainder of state spending grew by about 60 percent. Thus, even after the Massachusetts state treasury relieved a significant portion of the fiscal pressure placed on cities and towns by Proposition 2½, the growth of state revenues was enough to sustain an almost 60 percent expansion in real spending over the decade. Massachusetts' state budget was one of the fastest growing in the country; the average state budget grew by only about 40 percent in real terms.

In spite of increased state aid payments to local governments, real public expenditures by local governments in Massachusetts were

governments ensure that their revenues will cover their budgeted expenditures each year, resulting in a stable fiscal situation over time.

level; in the average state, real local spending increased by one-third. Thus, the combination of Proposition 2½ at the local level, an elastic revenue base at the state level, and a rapidly expanding economy led to a rapid relative decline in real local spending (as compared to other states) and a rapid increase in state spending (again as compared to other states). If expenditures financed by state aid to local governments are included in *state* spending, the disparity is even more dramatic.

The result was the largest shift in the state-local spending balance to occur nationwide. Figure 1-2 shows a chart of the states distributed by the shift in state government spending as a percentage of combined state and local governmental spending over the course of the decade. The share of combined state and local spending financed by state government rose in Massachusetts from about 40 percent to about 60 percent. As Figure 1-2 shows, this is substantially greater than the increase in any other state. The federal share also declined markedly, falling from about 30 percent to about 15 percent.

In 1979, three roughly equal partners financed public spending in Massachusetts. By 1989, the state government had emerged as the dominant force, more than twice the size of either of its two junior partners.

The Shift in Spending Priorities

What effect did the shift in the state-local spending balance have on the composition of spending? Was the allocation of overall state and local spending more or less stable across the decade, in spite of the change in the level of government collecting and distributing the funds? Or did local spending items lose ground with the decline in local financing, while state items gained?

This study shows that there was a substantial shift in the relative priority shown toward different spending areas. Broadly speaking, spending areas traditionally funded by local government were accorded a declining priority over the course of the decade. Elementary and secondary education expenditures, for example, are distributed

Figure 1-2
Percent Change in State Share of Spending
(before transfers)

1979–1989

-4	-2	0	2	4	6	8	10	12	14	16	18	20
		ID	NM									
		MI	AZ									
		IN	FL									
		PA	HI									
		UT	AL									
		WI	NE									
		SD	NH									
		NY	VA									
KY		CO	NC	AR								
OR	TN	MD	OH	WA								
TX	CA	LA	SC	ND	ME	MT						
MS	WV	IA	GA	RI	VT	DE						
MN	OK	KS	IL	MO	WY	NJ	CT	NV			MA	

Percent Change

at the local level. Compared with other states, the priority Massachusetts showed toward K–12 schooling declined sharply across the decade. By contrast, Massachusetts increased the relative priority it showed toward *higher* education, and it increased the relative priority it showed toward various areas of human services spending; both higher education and human services are financed largely from the state level.

One reading of this history is that the forces generated by the combination of Proposition 2½ at the local level and an income-elastic tax revenue base at the state level reflect a set of deliberate, changing public services tastes in Massachusetts. Under this reading, Proposition 2½ was designed not only to reduce local revenues in general, but expenditures on public schools in particular. The income-elasticity of the state tax base could also be interpreted as a result of conscious design—after all, the state could have cut tax rates (even more than it did) instead of increasing spending as the buoyant economy lifted state tax revenues. Instead, for the most part, Massachusetts left its income-elastic state tax system in place as the economy boomed and generated sufficient funds to finance additional human services expenditures.

While this reading is certainly possible, it ascribes a high degree of coordination to political forces working at very different levels of government and through very different institutions. More likely, these results had nothing at all to do with any grand political action plan developed or operated by any cohesive group. The results flowed from an at least partly accidental confluence of pressures, the natural evolution of a set of institutions and forces put in place by different interests working to advance different purposes. Two very different coalitions of political activists, working in essentially opposite directions on quite different agendas, one conservative and one liberal, both succeeded. Conservatives succeeded with Proposition 2½ at the local level (where the tax base was relatively insensitive to economic expansion, and revenues were not growing very rapidly); this resulted in a reduction of the priority exhibited toward elementary and secondary education. Liberals succeeded at the state level (where revenues were growing, making spending easier to expand); they increased the priority exhibited in combined state and local spending toward human services. The result of this confluence of forces was a substantial change, not in the overall level of public spending, but in its composition.

Spending Choices

The budget debate turns on a set of fundamental choices about political and social values. How much can we afford, and how much do we want to spend? How much should we emphasize physical and human investments in infrastructure and education, and how much should we emphasize current services? Which services are essential, and who should receive them? Which services should be provided publicly and which left to individuals to provide for themselves?

Questions of values are hard to debate in the abstract. What is the *right* amount of publicly provided education, health care, cash assistance, or infrastructure investment? Generally, people find it easiest to frame issues like these in terms of whether we should have more or less than we currently have. To know what direction they would prefer to move, taxpayers and public leaders need to begin with a good description of where we are today. What values *currently* are reflected in our public spending? How much do we *now* emphasize education, or cash assistance to the indigent, or services to mentally handicapped people?

The purpose of this study is to provide an anchor for the budget debate—to trace what our apparent priorities are and how they have changed over the course of the last decade, so that we can determine where we want to go from here. If we know where we are starting, we can choose which way to turn.

Previous Comparative Studies of State Spending

Total or per capita spending figures alone are not sufficient to describe meaningfully where we are today. To put the figures in perspective, they need to be viewed against a comparative backdrop. An obvious (and widely used) backdrop is other states' spending. In response to the unprecedented fiscal problems confronting Massachusetts, a number of analysts have compared the situation in Massachusetts with that in other states. These comparisons provide a sense of where Massachusetts stands as compared with all other states or with selected groups of other states.[3]

While they are insightful, previous studies generally share two important flaws that impede their use as a point of departure for the identification of political and social values reflected in public spending

---

3 For two excellent examples, see the Massachusetts Taxpayers Foundation, *State Budget Trends,* Boston, various years, and the Governor's Management Task Force, *Massachusetts: Managing Our Future,* Boston, 1990. Each provides a broad and useful array of comparisons.

policies. First, they generally do not allow for the cost of producing public services in Massachusetts, which is substantially higher than in many other states because both wages and living costs are higher in Massachusetts, driving up the cost of inputs needed to produce public services. Second, they typically compare Massachusetts to all other states, or to selected groups of states, with markedly different circumstances. Due to these differences, Massachusetts' spending should be expected to differ from that of the other states to which it is compared. Studies based on raw per capita figures can provide little or no guidance about how much of a difference should be expected. Therefore, it is difficult to tell whether the noted differences reflect a different pattern of priorities, or merely differences in the underlying circumstances.

States differ from one another in ways that can be expected to have significant effects on public spending. First and foremost, they differ in the costs they face to produce public services. Health care costs in Massachusetts, for example, are considerably above the national average. When the state seeks to provide a given level of real health care services to the poor, the expenditures required are higher than those in states with more moderate health resource costs. Beyond differences in costs, states differ in the characteristics that determine the need for public services. They differ, for example, in the number of poor and elderly in need of public assistance, in the number of school-age children in public schools and college students in the state's public higher education system, and in the concentration of the population in urban areas. Finally, beyond costs and needs, they differ in the affluence of their citizens, which influences the level of spending regarded as desirable.

Given the disparities in the underlying factors that influence the need and demand for public services, it is no wonder that spending on public services varies widely across states. Expected differences in spending, however, make it difficult to interpret the actual pattern of differences observed. To what extent are they the result of differing *conditions* that drive public spending? To what extent do they reflect differing *choices* about values and priorities?

The Approach

This study develops a new framework for comparing public spending across states. The goal is to describe public spending in Massachusetts and to identify the relative value choices embodied in the state's spending policies. First, data on public spending are adjusted using indices of the relative cost of the inputs required to produce them. This removes variations created by differing costs of provision among states.

Ideally, the next step would be to adjust spending figures in each state, in each spending area, and in each time period by a measure of the relative efficiency of public spending at that location and time in that area of spending. This would allow comparisons of the level of services actually provided across states and across time. Unfortunately, no reliable and consistent data on the relative efficiency of public service provision exist for *any* spending area across states and across time. There is, therefore, no way to adjust for the fact that some states may spend their funds more efficently, obtaining a higher level of services for each dollar spent. As a result, this study compares purchasing power expended across different states and time periods. If spending efficiency is constant across states and time, this will track the level of services actually provided. If spending efficiency varies widely—that is, if different states turn a dollar of (input-cost-adjusted) spending into significantly different levels of service provided—then this study should be understood as focusing on public service spending effort, rather than on services provided.

To provide a baseline for comparison, the pattern of input-cost-adjusted spending across states in each area of public service provision is examined as a function of underlying determinants of fiscal needs (such as the poverty rate, the size of the school-age population, and the fraction of people over age 65). Other determinants of the level of public spending (in particular, the level of personal income in the state and a series of measures designed to capture the effect of variations in the political cultures of different states) are included in this step as well. Finally, the observed national spending pattern is used to form a "benchmark" level of expected spending for Massachusetts. Massachusetts' specific fiscal and income circumstances are incorporated into the benchmark using the observed national pattern of how spending varies as those circumstances change.[4]

Since income is included as an explanatory variable in setting the benchmark, variations in public spending that result from differences in income across states are absorbed into the benchmark (rather than being included as part of the difference between the benchmark and actual spending). In effect, income is treated as a "circumstance" in this analysis, with the benchmark set for Massachusetts on the basis of its actual per capita income. The benchmark has been set on the basis of how much Massachusetts would be expected to spend if it shared the other states' value choices and shared their pattern of spending variations as a function of circumstances (including income levels).[5]

The observed pattern of variation in spending as a function of differences in political culture is *not* incorporated into the formulation of the benchmark. Political culture is treated as one of the value

---

4 Appendix A provides a detailed discussion of the methodology underlying the estimation of the benchmark spending relationships used in this study. Those who wish to examine the methodology in greater technical detail should turn to appendix A after reading this introductory chapter.

5 This interpretation is consistent with that normally used by economists in expenditure analyses, where preferences or values are separated from income, which is regarded as a circumstance. The alternative would be to set benchmarks as if each state had the average income, leaving the effect of income on spending as part of each state's "choices." Since income is an important determinant of public spending levels, the effect of this approach for Massachusetts in most spending areas would be to increase the gap between actual and benchmark spending. This would require repeated explanations that a large portion of the gap is attributable to Massachusetts' high income. This issue is discussed in more detail in appendix A.

choices that drives public spending, not as a need or circumstance beyond the control of the people of the state. The benchmark for Massachusetts is formed as if the state had the *average* political culture of the other states. Thus, the difference between the benchmark and the actual spending observed in Massachusetts includes differences attributable to its political predispositions.

The benchmark estimated for each area of public service provision should not be interpreted as the amount Massachusetts *should* be spending. Massachusetts should spend whatever levels taxpayers choose, based upon *their* values. The benchmark embodies the average value choices observed in other states, adjusted to reflect Massachusetts' specific conditions. Massachusetts taxpayers' values are not necessarily the same as those of the other states taken together—indeed, there are many reasons (such as the pattern of Massachusetts' voting in national elections) to think that the pattern of value choices may be different from that of other states. These effects, captured by the political culture measures, are interpreted as a component of the value choices made (explicitly or implicitly) by the people of Massachusetts.

Using the benchmark, Massachusetts can be differentiated from states that are known to be systematically different. Massachusetts' actual spending may be compared with the expected level of spending that would result *if* Massachusetts made the same value choices as the average of those made by the other states and *if* it followed the observed national pattern of how spending varies as a result of changes in underlying conditions (the poverty rate, income, and so on). This makes more sense than comparing Massachusetts to all other states (a collection that differs markedly from Massachusetts in income, sociodemographic composition, and resource costs), or to a selected group of states (which will still differ importantly from Massachusetts). This comparison—of Massachusetts' actual public spending, area by area, to the estimated benchmark—highlights the pattern of choices implicit in Massachusetts' spending, how it differs from that of other states, and also how it has shifted over time. The difference between actual and benchmark spending will show Massachusetts' spending priorities relative to those that other states would show, on average, if they were in Massachusetts' circumstances.

Components

To form the benchmark, specific variables that reflect fiscal circumstances and political culture must be chosen, and the variables must be distinguished on the basis of whether they measure fiscal circumstances or political culture. For example, the party affiliation of the governor might influence the level of spending, but it almost surely reflects political and social values rather than any meaningful fiscal need. This factor therefore should be used to capture part of the value choices the state makes about spending. By contrast, the poverty rate in the state reflects a need that can be expected to drive public spending, and should be treated as a fiscal need indicator in the pattern of spending across states.

Different decisions about exactly which variables to include—which are cast as reflections of political culture, tastes, and values, and which are cast as needs driving public spending—would result in some variation in the benchmark for every state. Choices about how to measure the included variables—for example, measuring income per capita, or income per family—will also have some impact on the benchmarks. Since the benchmark for each state is an estimate formed from a particular set of decisions—about which variables to include in the analysis, whether to classify variables under political culture or fiscal need, and how to measure them—benchmarks are not immutable or precisely measured.

Forming estimates of what each state would spend on the basis of spending observed in other states requires data that are consistently developed across all states included in the study.[6] Since states make

---

6 Alaska was excluded from all analysis and comparisons that follow because its spending patterns and circumstances are so radically different from those of other states.

widely differing choices about which level of government (state or local) should conduct which components of spending, the focus here is on combined state and local government spending. The study uses the most reliable comparative data available, those published annually by the Federal Bureau of the Census. It examines the period from 1979 to 1989 (the latest year for which the federal data are available).

The Bureau of the Census provides highly disaggregated data covering a wide variety of narrowly defined spending areas, many of which are of limited interest in forming a general view of the value choices made by state and local governments as a whole. This study concentrates on the most important broad areas of spending with particular interest for the state's ongoing debate about public spending values.

Education. The largest area of combined state and local spending and the largest employer of public workers, education includes all non-capital expenditures for the maintenance and operation of public schools. For purposes of this study, it is divided into two categories: 1) elementary and secondary education (grades K–12), and 2) postsecondary education.

Human Services. The largest area of state spending, this includes the major programs for the support of the poor and the mentally or physically handicapped. Its two largest components are direct assistance to individuals[7] and spending on health and hospitals (public health programs and payments for hospitalization and residential care for mentally ill and mentally retarded people). These two components, which constitute the bulk of human services spending, are studied separately.

---

7 The Census data on which this study is based refer to this area as "public welfare." Since this area includes not only traditional welfare payments, but also the large and rapidly growing Medicaid program, it will be described here under the more comprehensive label "direct assistance to individuals."

Highways. An area of significant public works and physical investment activity, this area includes operating expenditures on highway operation and maintenance, and capital investment expenditures. Operations spending and total spending (including capital expenditures) are each analyzed because capital spending variability over time makes states' spending in any given year not fully comparable to one another.

Public Safety and Corrections. These two areas are examined separately in the study. Public safety includes expenditures for police and fire services and preventive activities. Corrections includes expenditures for construction, maintenance, and operation of incarceration facilities.

General Expenditures. The most inclusive category, this area encompasses essentially all expenditures other than payments to the federal government.

Organization of the Study

The five core chapters of this study review specific areas of spending in detail, examining the pattern of changes in relative emphasis and exploring the reasons why Massachusetts' spending in each area differs from the national average and how it changed between 1979 and 1989. Chapter 2 takes up education. Chapter 3 examines the major areas of spending in human services: direct assistance and health and hospitals. Chapter 4 probes spending on highway operations. Chapter 5 explores public safety and corrections expenditures. Chapter 6 examines general operating expenditures. Chapter 7 summarizes the results, and suggests how they might be used to help recast the ongoing debate about public spending in the Commonwealth.

For those interested in the technical details of the methods developed and applied here, the appendices form an integral part of this report. Appendix A provides an extended discussion of the methodology, a technical description of the benchmark estimation process, and a detailed examination of how the results will be presented. Appendix B provides a lengthy description of the data, the data sources, and the process of adjusting the expenditure data for input-cost variations. Appendix C provides the estimated coefficients from the expenditure pattern analyses used to estimate the benchmarks. Those who want a deeper acquaintance with the approach to establishing benchmarks than the intuitive description provided in this chapter should read appendix A before proceeding to the core chapters that follow.

CHAPTER TWO

Public Education

Expenditures on public education are the largest component of state and local government spending. Shifts in spending on education are thus crucial determinants of the overall pattern and level of state and local spending.[1]

A quick examination of Massachusetts' apparent experience—based on comparing Massachusetts to the national average in terms of nominal spending[2]—would reveal little change in the relation between the Commonwealth's and the rest of the country's spending on local elementary and secondary education over the course of the past decade. Proposition 2½ notwithstanding, per student spending remained considerably above the national average. In fact, the gap between Massachusetts' nominal per student spending and that of the rest of the nation increased from about $600 per student in 1979 to

---

1 This chapter focuses on the *operating* expenditures for public education, leaving aside capital spending. Capital spending varies considerably from year to year as large projects are undertaken or completed; focusing on operating spending directs attention toward the ongoing provision of public education services. Perhaps the best focus for analysis would be operating spending plus a measure of capital spending averaged across several years, but the available data do not allow such an analysis for the period of this study.

2 The word "nominal" refers to figures that are *not* adjusted for inflation across time or for regional differences in input costs or prices. Thus, nominal spending of $100 in 1980 refers to the disbursement of the same number of dollars, but a different level of purchasing power, than nominal spending of $100 in 1989. In this study, figures are generally reported in cost-adjusted terms, referred to as "real" terms, except where it is explicitly noted that unadjusted (nominal) figures are used.

over $1100 by 1989. In higher education, a look at nominal spending suggests that the Commonwealth began the decade considerably below the national average in per student spending, but quickly moved up through the ranks, climbing above the national average in 1989. Its rank leaped from 48th to 22d out of 49 states (leaving out Alaska).

The story suggested by nominal spending figures is misleading. It obscures a steady rise in the national average of per student spending, in part due to increased costs nationwide. It ignores Massachusetts' input costs, which are substantially higher than the national average (it costs more to maintain an equivalent school, to heat it, and to pay teachers in Massachusetts than in most states). Both of these factors significantly alter the story about Massachusetts—and about what changed in the 1980s.

An accurate assessment of education spending reveals that the emphasis Massachusetts placed on per student operating spending for elementary and secondary education dropped significantly; in real, cost-adjusted terms, the Commonwealth's rank changed from 1st to 21st in the relative priority placed on K–12 education. In higher education, the state did increase its rank but remained well below the average, moving only from 48th to 41st.

As in most states, elementary and secondary education spending in Massachusetts is conducted at the local level. Through local aid payments, the state carries some of the burden of this local spending, but at the margin most communities in the state are limited in what they can spend by Proposition 2½. By contrast, higher education is financed through the state level, so it must compete with other state-level priorities. Perhaps as a result, the pattern of spending on elementary and secondary education has shifted in very different ways over the last decade than the spending pattern on higher education.

Public Elementary and Secondary Education

Forming the Benchmark

The need for spending on elementary and secondary education is primarily driven by the number of students enrolled in public schools. As a result, the benchmark for spending on education is defined in terms of spending per enrolled student. What factors should be expected to influence the level of spending per student? Since input cost variations (for example, the level of wages prevailing in the state's labor market) have been removed before this part of the analysis started, remaining factors have to do with the differential needs of (or costs associated with teaching) different segments of the population. The analysis presented here allowed for differences across states in the prevalence of poverty and in the degree of concentration of population in metropolitan areas. Also, unusually high student enrollment levels might allow schools to reduce the amount spent on each student; as a consequence, the level of public school enrollment in the state was included as an explanatory variable. Finally, as in all the analyses, a measure of income and a time trend were included.[3]

The Dispersion of Priorities

During the 1980s, Massachusetts moved from having the nation's highest relative priority on public elementary and secondary education to being approximately in the middle of the national distribution. Figure 2-1 shows the distribution of priorities for 1979 and for 1989. Here, the difference between each state's actual spending and its own benchmark is taken as the measure of the relative priority the state is showing toward K–12 education. Figure 2-1 can be thought of as a distribution of the states, arrayed in terms of the implicit choices they make about how much to spend on public elementary and secondary

---

3   The precise specification of all explanatory variables used in each spending area is found in appendix C, together with the results of the regression estimates of the benchmark spending relationships.

Figure 2-1

Elementary and Secondary Education Operating Expenditures per Pupil
Difference from Benchmark (in 1989 dollars)

1979

Dollars	States
1000+	MA (boxed)
800	NY
700	RI, NJ
400	MD, NM
300	CA, WI
200	OR, UT
0	MN, MT, CT, PA, ND, MI, FL, AZ, CO
-100	NE, DE, IA, WY
-200	WA, NC, OH, VA
-300	IL, HI, SD, LA, TX
-400	ME, MS, VT, SC, GA, NV, KS
-500	AL, MO
-700	IN, AR, TN, WV, OK
-800	NH, KY
-1000	ID

Axis: -1000 -900 -800 -700 -600 -500 -400 -300 -200 -100 0 100 200 300 400 500 600 700 800 900 1000+   Dollars

1989

Dollars	States
1000+	WY, NY, OR
800	NJ
700	WI
600	RI
500	PA
400	MT
300	NE
200	CT
100	VT, MN
0	IA, FL, DE
-100	MI, OH, CO, ND, WA
-200	MA (boxed), MD, NM, SD, TX, VA
-300	KS, ME, NC, UT, CA
-400	SC, AZ, IN
-500	GA, MO
-600	WV, LA, MS
-700	OK, NH
-800	NV, AR, IL, AL
-1000	TN, KY, HI, ID

Axis: -1000 -900 -800 -700 -600 -500 -400 -300 -200 -100 0 100 200 300 400 500 600 700 800 900 1000+   Dollars education (as compared to the 49 sample states). States on the far left side of the distribution have actual spending substantially below what would be predicted based on other states' behavior; these states are showing relatively low priority for public K–12 education. Those states on the far right side of the distribution have spending considerably in excess of what would be expected based on other states; these states are showing a high relative emphasis on public elementary and secondary education. In 1979, no state showed a higher spending priority on K–12 education than Massachusetts, which was spending $900 more per student than its benchmark. By 1989, twenty states showed higher priorities than Massachusetts (controlling for the differences in their circumstances), and actual spending had dropped to $200 below the expected benchmark.[4]

Pattern of Massachusetts' Relative Priority over Time

Figure 2-2 tracks the shift in Massachusetts' spending on elementary and secondary school education in the 1980s. Actual elementary and secondary public school spending (in real 1989 dollars for all years) is contrasted with the benchmark for Massachusetts for 1979 to 1989 based on the 49 sample states. At the beginning of the period, Massachusetts' spending was about $900 per student higher than would have been expected given its then-prevailing circumstances. Between 1979 and 1982, real spending in Massachusetts on elementary and secondary education declined, while rising incomes (and a general pattern of increases in real spending observed in other states) combined to create an expected increase of about $500 in spending per enrolled student. From 1982 to 1985, real spending was approximately constant—while the benchmark again rose by $500 per student. By 1984, spending in Massachusetts was somewhat lower than would have been expected given its circumstances. From 1986

---

4   Appendix A provides a more detailed description of how the figures and tables presented in this study were computed and how they can be interpreted (see the section titled "Reporting the Results").

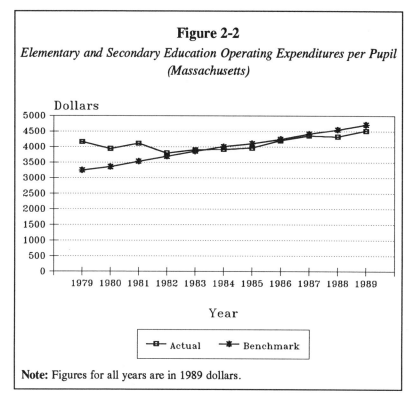

Figure 2-2

Elementary and Secondary Education Operating Expenditures per Pupil
(Massachusetts)

Note: Figures for all years are in 1989 dollars.

to 1989, spending per enrolled student in Massachusetts increased at about the same rate as the benchmark, closing the period below what would be expected on the basis of its circumstances.

Understanding the Difference between Massachusetts and the National Average

How can it be that in 1989 Massachusetts was spending more than the national average (in nominal terms) but spending less than its benchmark (in real terms)? There are two major parts to the answer. First, costs in Massachusetts are high—and even high spending in the face of high costs provides only a moderate level of service. Second, Massachusetts' income by 1989 was high, and since states with higher incomes are expected to spend more, Massachusetts had a high benchmark or expected spending. By 1989, Massachusetts' real spending on public elementary and secondary education was about $200 per enrolled student, about 5 percent, below what would be expected on the basis of its circumstances. Its nominal spending was about 12 percent higher than the national average. Table 2-1 shows the components of difference between Massachusetts' nominal spending in 1989 and the national average. Essentially all of the difference in nominal spending is accounted for by the fact that Massachusetts faces higher input costs than the average state. Additional spending of about 1 percent of the national average is expected as a result of

Table 2-1

Reconciliation of National Average to Massachusetts Spending Public Elementary and Secondary Education Operating Spending per Enrolled Student, 1989

	Spending per enrolled student (1989 dollars)	Percent of national average
National average spending		
Nominal national average	4554	100
Adjustment to national average		
for Massachusetts input costs	597	13
Differences in circumstances		
Fiscal need indicators	110	2
Per capita income	51	1
Input costs associated with		
differences due to circumstances	21	0
Differences in choices		
Choice differences	-200	-4
Input costs associated with		
differences due to choices	-26	-1
Nominal Massachusetts 1989		
spending	5105	112

the fact that Massachusetts has considerably higher income than the average state.

Understanding the Change in Massachusetts' Elementary and Secondary Education Spending, 1979–1989

Table 2-2 shows the components of the real spending change over the period. If the state had held constant the relative priority it was showing in 1979 toward K–12 public education—that is, if state spending increased only because of changes in fiscal need indicators (such as the number of students enrolled), per capita income, and the general national time trend—spending per enrolled student would have been expected to rise by about $1450, from $4160 in 1979 to about $5600 in 1989. About $900 of this change would have been expected to have been generated by the general time trend of increasing real education spending observed nationwide.

Table 2-2
Analysis of 1979–1989 Change in Real Massachusetts Spending
Public Elementary and Secondary Education Operating Spending per
Enrolled Student

	Spending per enrolled student (1989 dollars)	Percent of 1979 spending
Massachusetts 1979 real spending	4158	100
1979–1989 changes in circumstances		
Change in fiscal need indicators	468	11
Change in per capita income	105	3
General time trend and changes in national choices	894	21
1979–1989 changes in choices	-1111	-27
Massachusetts 1989 real spending	4514	109

Instead, Massachusetts' spending rose, in real terms, only by about $350 per enrolled student during this period. Massachusetts' relative priority for elementary and secondary education did not hold constant, but shifted *downward* by over $1100 per student, substantially reducing the actual increase observed in Massachusetts as compared to what would have been expected.

The quick examination of nominal spending, which suggested that the Commonwealth's spending on K–12 education continued upward unaffected by Proposition 2½, proved to sketch a false picture. Instead, the substantial drop in available local revenues, in spite of additional assistance from Commonwealth coffers, correlated with an $1100 per student drop in the priority shown toward elementary and secondary education.

Public Higher Education

Forming the Benchmark

As with elementary and secondary education, an appropriate focus of the analysis of public higher education expenditures is the spending per student, and the analysis rests on similar factors.[5] With the exception of the poverty rate, the explanatory variables included to form the benchmark were the same as with K–12 education. As in the case of K–12 education, there may be different costs associated with providing higher education in heavily urbanized areas, so the

---

5   An alternative approach would be to focus on spending per college-age state resident. If some states restrict entry but spend a large amount per enrolled student, they will appear to have a high priority toward higher education, and this may seem anomalous. Focusing on spending per college-age resident would adjust for this problem, but it introduces two other anomalies: 1) Many state higher education systems educate students who are not "college-age," and 2) states differ widely in how much they rely on private higher education institutions as part of their overall education strategy. Because Massachusetts has a virtually unrivalled private higher education system, it seems appropriate to explore its effort in terms of spending per student actually enrolled in the public system.

explanatory variables include the percentage of the population living in metropolitan areas. Since having a larger public higher education system enrollment may change the spending per student, it was entered as an explanatory variable. Income and the general time trend were also included. Poverty should be less relevant for higher than for K–12 education because students are prepared for college through the elementary and secondary school systems, so their families' economic conditions may be expected to have less of an impact.

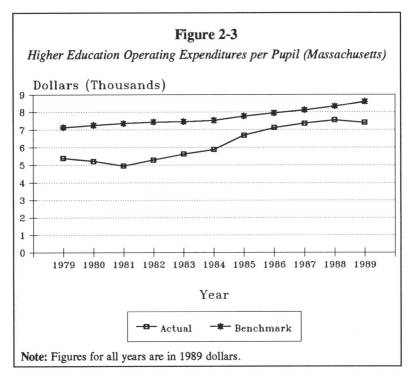

Figure 2-3

Higher Education Operating Expenditures per Pupil (Massachusetts)

Note: Figures for all years are in 1989 dollars.

Pattern of Massachusetts' Relative Priority over Time

Figure 2-3 shows the benchmark and actual spending (both in real 1989 dollars for all years) for Massachusetts from 1979 to 1989 based on the 49 sample states. Massachusetts began the period according a relatively low priority to higher education. The Commonwealth spent nearly $1750 per enrolled student less than would be expected given its then-prevailing income and other circumstances. Between 1979 and 1981, real spending on higher education declined in Massachusetts on a per-enrolled-student basis, further diverging from the benchmark, which was rising with the national time trend. However, Massachusetts reversed its downward trend in the period from 1981 to 1988, with real spending per enrolled student rising from less than $5000 in 1981 to over $7500 in 1988. In 1989, real spending declined slightly. By the end of the period, Massachusetts was spending about $1200, about 14 percent, less per enrolled student than the benchmark would predict for a state with its circumstances.

The Dispersion of Priorities

In 1979, Massachusetts stood 48th out of the 49 sample states in terms of its actual spending on higher education per enrolled student in comparison to its benchmark. Figure 2-4 shows the distribution of states according to their actual 1989 spending in comparison to their individual benchmarks. In 1989, in spite of the increase in its spending, Massachusetts still showed lower priority toward higher education spending per student than 40 of the 49 states in the sample.

The 49 sample states show a relatively wide dispersion of priorities toward public higher education, with some states spending as much as $3000 per student below their benchmarks while others spend as much as $4000 per student more than would be anticipated. This reflects a rather broad range of strategies selected by different states. Viewed this way, by 1989 Massachusetts was less of an extreme departure from the bulk of other states than it had been in 1979.

Understanding the Difference between Massachusetts and the National Average

How, specifically, did Massachusetts' higher education spending differ from the national average? Which factors driving spending had the most impact? Table 2-3 shows a reconciliation of Massachusetts' actual 1989 spending per enrolled higher education student with the

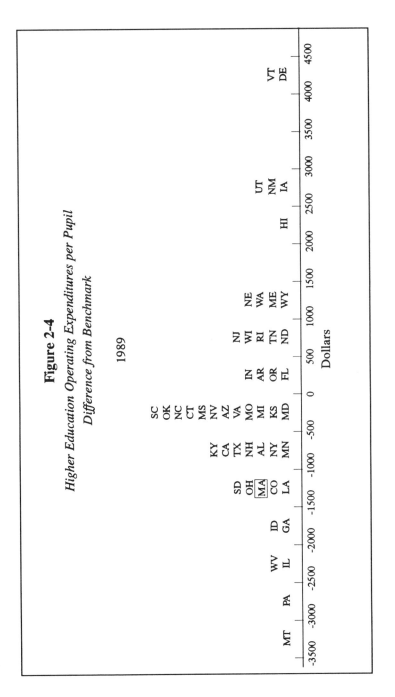

Figure 2-4

Higher Education Operating Expenditures per Pupil

Difference from Benchmark

Table 2-3

Reconciliation of National Average to Massachusetts Spending
Public Higher Education Operating Spending per
Enrolled Student, 1989

	Spending per enrolled student (1989 dollars)	
	All Operating Expenditures	State Spending Net of Tuition Charges and Federal Reimbursement
National average spending		
Nominal national average	9304	4842
Adjustment to national average for Massachusetts input costs	1229	646
Differences in circumstances		
Fiscal need indicators	-523	17
Per capita income	-178	309
Input costs associated with differences due to circumstances	-93	44
Differences in choices		
Choice differences	-1196	-1024
Input costs associated with differences due to choices	-158	-137
Nominal Massachusetts 1989 spending	8385	4696

national average. The nominal national average was about $9300 per student; Massachusetts in 1989 spent about $8400. Adding the higher input costs faced by Massachusetts to the national average would produce equivalent spending of about $10,500 per student; adjusting for Massachusetts' income and fiscal need circumstances would reduce this by about $800.[6] In all, Massachusetts might have been expected to spend about $9700 per student (in nominal terms). Its actual spending thus fell below what would be expected in nominal terms by about $1350 per student.

Table 2-3 also shows a reconciliation of Massachusetts' spending to the national average absent student charges (notably tuition) and federal reimbursements. The operating expenditures column represents the full package of services experienced by students in the Commonwealth's higher education system; the net column shows what the Commonwealth itself spent in support of its students enrolled in public higher education. Tuition charges make up a substantial portion—about a third—of higher education funding in virtually all states, and Massachusetts is no exception.

It is noteworthy that the gap between predicted and actual spending is roughly the same whether the focus is on total operating expenditures or on expenditures net of federal reimbursements and charges (approximately $1200 and $1025, respectively). This parity indicates that the gap between actual and benchmark spending lies principally in the level of state financing; tuition and federal reimbursement each contribute roughly what would be expected, but the state's relatively low contribution results in low overall operating expenditures in comparison with the anticipated spending level.

Understanding the Change in Massachusetts' Higher Education Spending, 1979–1989

The priority Massachusetts accorded to higher education, compared to what would be expected based on what other states do, was

---

6   In contrast to the other estimated benchmark relationships, in this equation per capita income has a negative effect. This may reflect an anomaly in the estimation, or it may correctly reflect a true phenomenon. It is possible, for example, that in wealthier states the better students go to private schools, reducing the propensity of the state to make investments in the students who attend public universities.

relatively low in 1989, but rose between 1979 and 1989. Table 2-4 shows the components of the increase in Massachusetts' spending on higher education across the period. Massachusetts' real spending on higher education rose by about $2000 per student across the period, from about $5400 to about $7400. The overall change in circumstances was driven largely by the general observed national time trend. The $550 increase in relative priority accorded to higher education was offset by declines caused by circumstances and income, so that the overall increase in Massachusetts was nearly identical to the national increase over time.

Table 2-4
Decomposition of 1979–1989 Change in Real Massachusetts Spending
Public Higher Education Operating Spending per Enrolled Student

	Spending per enrolled student (1989 dollars)	Percent of 1979 spending
Massachusetts 1979 real spending	5395	100
1979–1989 changes in circumstances		
Change in fiscal need indicators	-141	-3
Change in per capita income	-366	-7
General time trend	1969	36
1979–1989 changes in choices	550	10
Massachusetts 1989 real spending	7407	137

Commentary

It should be noted that Massachusetts has a very robust *private* education system, at the elementary and secondary as well as at the higher education levels. As a result, the measures presented here of the relative priority accorded to public education efforts do not encompass the full effort made by taxpayers in the state toward the education of their children. The focus of the analysis here, however, is not total spending but spending per enrolled student. Massachusetts may be expected to spend less overall on public education because it sends fewer students through public schools, but there is no obvious reason to expect that it would spend any less *per enrolled public school student* than do other states. Of course, the fact that many Massachusetts families enroll their children in private schools may reduce their willingness to support public education. Since the parents of publicly enrolled schoolchildren are often a potent political force in sustaining education as a high public spending priority, their absence may be an important influence determining the relatively low priority Massachusetts showed toward public K–12 education by 1989. It does little, however, to explain the major downward shift in the priority shown toward this area across the decade.

It should also be noted that these aggregate state and local government spending figures may mask important shifts in relative priority across different areas of any given state. For example, Massachusetts made a strong effort to focus additional resources on school districts in poorer, urban communities during the 1980s; such shifts among the Commonwealth's school districts would not be visible in the data examined here.

Whatever shifts may have occurred internally, there was a substantial shift in the aggregate priority Massachusetts showed toward education. In 1979, Massachusetts placed a higher priority on elementary and secondary education than any other state—and a lower priority on higher education than any state except Pennsylvania. Over the next ten years, the state's relative spending priority moved toward the national median in both areas. It seems no mere coincidence that K–12 spending, which fell substantially in its movement toward the median, is conducted at the level of government that is subject to relatively inelastic revenue growth and to Proposition 2½ ,while higher education spending, which increased toward the median, is conducted at the state level, where revenues grew rapidly across the decade.[7]

---

7   It should be noted, however, that much of the decline in K–12 spending in comparison to its benchmark was completed by 1982, the first year in which Proposition 2 1/2 legally applied to local spending. Perhaps some of the groundswell of political support for the proposition was reflected in local spending decisions even before it legally applied. Public officials knew that it had passed by early November 1980 (early in fiscal year 1981), and so may have begun adjusting to its impacts to some extent before they were legally bound by it. Alternatively, the decline may be explained by some other phenomenon entirely.

CHAPTER THREE

Human Services

After expenditures on public education, human services spending is the largest component of state and local government spending. This study examines the two largest components of human services spending, direct assistance programs and spending on health and hospitals.[1] Together, these two areas of human services spending make up about one-fifth of state and local spending, and about 98 percent of human services spending.

Direct assistance includes Aid to Families with Dependent Children (AFDC) and other cash assistance programs, as well as Medicaid and other health services provided directly to those enrolled in assistance programs. Thus, it comprises both the welfare system as commonly understood *and* health care for the elderly and poor.[2]

The health and hospitals programs, by contrast, support the general public health and the construction and maintenance of public health facilities. Also covered are most mental health programs, encompassing both inpatient care in state institutions and contract services provided by private and nonprofit agencies.

---

1 In examining direct assistance programs, both capital and operating spending were included because separate capital expenditure data are not available in this area over the whole study period. The amount of capital expenditures in this area is relatively small, however, so this should not affect the results materially. In the health and hospitals area, only operating spending was considered.

2 Ideally, traditional welfare programs would be analyzed separately from health care programs. Unfortunately, reliable data on each of the two components are not available for the whole study period.

In direct assistance programs, the federal government reimburses states for a large fraction of total expenditures. The reimbursement rates vary from state to state and across different spending areas, so states with different emphases within direct assistance are reimbursed somewhat differently. In Massachusetts' case, just short of half of all direct assistance spending conducted by the state has been reimbursed by the federal government. In health and hospitals programs, government agencies are reimbursed by third parties or paid directly by service recipients (through charges) for a substantial fraction of their activities. Thus, analysis can focus either on all expenditures, or on expenditures net of reimbursements and charges—that is, on the support contributed by state and local governments to these programs. The pattern of human services spending in Massachusetts as compared with other states is quite similar whether one considers total spending or spending out of state funds alone. Because the focus of this study is on state spending, the analysis here will concentrate primarily on net spending on human services programs, excluding federal reimbursements (for direct assistance programs) and charges (for health and hospitals programs).

Direct Assistance

In nominal terms, net state spending on direct assistance expanded abruptly over the decade, rising from about $1200 per poor person in 1979 to about $3200 per poor person in 1989, or by a factor of more than two and a half. Of the $2000 increase, about $900 represents the amount required to provide the same services after adjusting for national inflation. Massachusetts' actual inflation over the period was faster than the national average, accounting for an increase of a further $200 per poor person to provide the same real level of services as in 1979. The remaining $900 increase resulted from the higher real level of services Massachusetts provided in 1989.

Forming the Benchmark

The need for spending on the wide array of direct assistance programs is primarily driven by the number of people living in poverty. As a result, the benchmark for spending on direct assistance programs was defined in terms of spending per person living below the poverty level.[3] What factors should be expected to influence the level of spending per poor person? The data used for this analysis have already been adjusted for input cost variations (for example, the level of wages prevailing in the state's labor market), so remaining factors have to do with the differential needs of (or costs associated with providing services to) different segments of the population. By far the most important components of direct assistance spending are Medicaid and cash assistance payments. A large component of Medicaid spending goes to pay for nursing home care for indigent elderly people, so the ratio of elderly people in the state to poor people in the state was included as an explanatory influence. Cash assistance payments to poor families are concentrated among female-headed households, so the prevalence of such families and the ratio of young people to poor people were also included. The analysis also allowed

---

3 Published figures on the number of people living in poverty generally use the federal poverty line as the standard definition. The federal standard varies by family size, but not by location. Therefore, in states with high costs of living, estimates based on this standard can be expected to understate the number of people below the poverty line, and correspondingly to overstate it in states with low living costs. Accordingly, in this study the number of people reported to be living in poverty under the federal definition was adjusted to take account of local variations in the cost of living. The adjustments are described in more detail in Appendix B. Unfortunately, all figures based on the federal poverty definition count the number of poor *after* receipt of income from public programs. This means that a state whose income assistance program was exceptionally successful at lifting people out of poverty would have a very small number of remaining people in poverty and an exceptionally high value for expenditures per poor person. Ideally, data on the number of people who would be living in poverty in the absence of assistance programs would be used instead. No consistent data on this basis are available.

for differences across states in the concentration of population in metropolitan areas. Finally, as in all the analyses, a measure of income and a time trend were included.[4]

Pattern of Massachusetts' Relative Priority over Time

Figure 3-1 shows the benchmark and actual net Massachusetts state spending on direct assistance (in real 1989 dollars for all years) for 1979 to 1989 based on the 49 sample states. Spending in this area of human services exceeded the benchmark by a substantial margin throughout the period. In 1979, net state spending exceeded what would have been expected based on other states and Massachusetts'

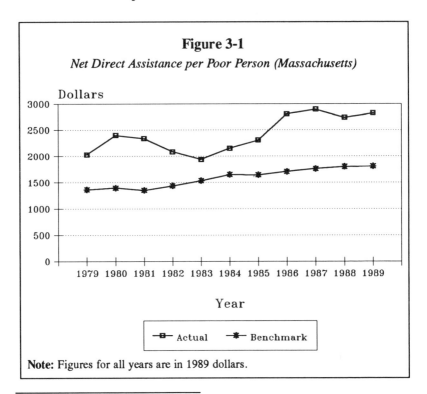

Figure 3-1

Net Direct Assistance per Poor Person (Massachusetts)

Note: Figures for all years are in 1989 dollars.

---

4 Appendix C provides the detailed specification of each variable used and presents the regression results.

then-current circumstances by about $700 per poor person. *Total* real spending per poor person was almost constant between 1979 and 1984; *net* state spending first rose and then fell in response to Reagan-era changes in federal reimbursement. Actual net state spending per poor person rose substantially in 1984, 1985 and 1986, and by 1989 the gap between actual and benchmark spending had widened to over $1000 per poor person.

The Dispersion of Priorities

Figure 3-2 shows charts of the difference between each state's net spending on direct assistance and its benchmark for 1979 and 1989. In both years, Massachusetts stood third among the states in terms of priority accorded to direct assistance relative to anticipated benchmarks.

Understanding the Difference between Massachusetts and the National Average

Nominal total spending on direct assistance programs in Massachusetts in 1989 was about $5900 per poor person, twice the national average of about $2900. Of the $5900, the state paid about $3200, nearly 2½ times as much as the average state paid out of its own funds. Table 3-1 provides a reconciliation of Massachusetts' net state spending and the national average for 1989. About $300 of the roughly $1900 per poor person difference was due to fiscal needs differences—notably, Massachusetts' high ratio of elderly population to people living in poverty and high number of female-headed households per poor person raised its anticipated costs in the Medicaid program and in direct assistance. About $200 of the difference was due to the fact that, as a higher-income state, Massachusetts can be expected to spend more per poor person on these types of public services. Nearly $400 more was attributable to Massachusetts' relatively high input costs. The remaining $1000 difference—nearly 80 percent of the national average by itself—was the difference between

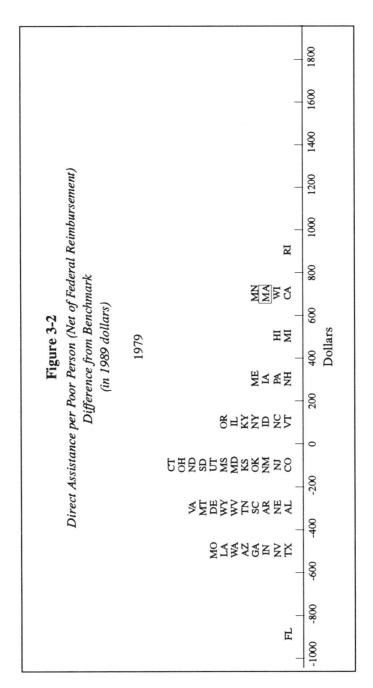

Figure 3-2

Direct Assistance per Poor Person (Net of Federal Reimbursement)

Difference from Benchmark

(in 1989 dollars)

1979

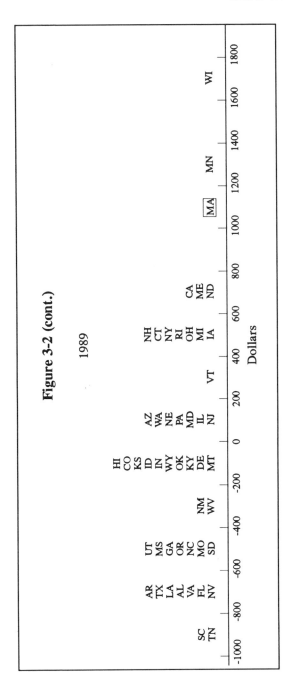

Figure 3-2 (cont.)

1989

Dollars

the expected benchmark and actual spending, showing the priority Massachusetts attributes to providing direct assistance.

Table 3-1

Reconciliation of National Average to Massachusetts Spending
Direct Assistance Net State Spending per Poor Person, 1989

	Spending per poor person (1989 dollars)	Percent of national average
National average spending		
Nominal national average	1326	100
Adjustment to national average		
for Massachusetts input costs	181	14
Differences in circumstances		
Fiscal need indicators	296	22
Per capita income	187	14
Input costs associated with		
differences due to circumstances	66	5
Differences in choices		
Choice differences	1017	77
Input costs associated with		
differences due to choices	139	10
Nominal Massachusetts 1989		
spending	3210	242

Understanding the Change in Massachusetts Direct Assistance Spending, 1979–1989

Table 3-2 shows the components of the change in Massachusetts' spending on direct assistance from 1979 to 1989. Over the course of the period, real spending in this area rose from about $2000 to about $2800 per poor person, or by about 40 percent. Two main factors drove this increase. The substantial increase in per capita income in Massachusetts across the period raised the benchmark by approxi-

Table 3-2

Analysis of 1979–1989 Change in Real Massachusetts Spending
Direct Assistance Net State Spending per Poor Person

	Spending per poor person (1989 dollars)	Percent of 1979 spending
Massachusetts 1979 real spending	2031	100
1979–1989 changes in circumstances		
Change in fiscal need indicators	87	4
Change in per capita income	385	19
General time trend and change in national choices	-28	-1
1979–1989 changes in choices	351	17
Massachusetts 1989 real spending	2825	139

mately $400, so with no further changes in circumstances or relative priority, spending would have been expected to rise to about $2450. The remaining difference of roughly $350 indicates an increase in relative priority. About 20 of the approximately 43 percentage point increase in spending stemmed from a change in what Massachusetts chose to spend on direct assistance.

Health and Hospitals

Net state spending on Massachusetts' health and hospitals programs rose rapidly across the decade in nominal terms, nearly tripling from $97 per capita in 1979 to $275 per capita in 1989. The expansion was particularly rapid from 1984 to 1989. Throughout the period, net health and hospitals spending substantially exceeded the national average. About half of the nearly $180 increase per capita was due to inflation; the other half represented an increase in the real level of funds expended.

Forming the Benchmark

Unlike the human services programs that aid only poor people, spending through some health and hospitals programs is broadly dispersed throughout the population. For example, spending on mental health, mental retardation, and other mental and physical disabilities is generally included under the aegis of health and hospitals programs, and there is no reason to expect that spending in these areas will be exclusively for poor people. In some states (including Massachusetts), such programs make up the bulk of net state spending on health and hospitals. In other states (notably those in the South), more general health care is provided through programs classified in this spending area.[5] The appropriate focus of the analysis for this spending area, therefore, is the level of spending per capita. The concentration of children and elderly people may, however, affect the level of need for these programs, and they were accordingly allowed for as spending influences. As in the case of other human services programs, different costs may be associated with providing health and hospitals services in heavily urbanized areas, so the explanatory variables include the percentage of the population living in metropolitan areas and the poverty rate. Income and a general time trend were also included.[6][7]

---

5   To the extent that these variations are regional, they will be adjusted for by the regional indicator variables included in the set of political culture variables in establishing the benchmark. Actual spending in each state is thus being compared to a benchmark that embodies the average regional choice for the composition and level of health and hospitals programs.

6   It is worth noting that disability, mental retardation, and other rates in the population potentially associated with spending in this area are *not* included in the estimation of the benchmark. This study assumes that the underlying rates are the same, and differences in measured rates reflect differences in choices about how to classify various conditions.

7   Appendix C sets out the detailed specification of each variable used in forming the benchmark, and presents the regression results.

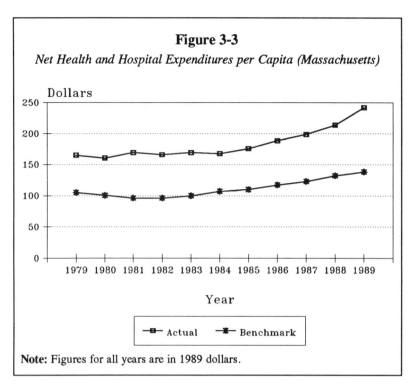

Figure 3-3

Net Health and Hospital Expenditures per Capita (Massachusetts)

Note: Figures for all years are in 1989 dollars.

Pattern of Massachusetts' Relative Priority over Time

Figure 3-3 shows the benchmark and actual net state spending on health and hospitals programs (both in real 1989 dollars for all years) for Massachusetts for 1979 to 1989 based on the 49 sample states. As was the case for direct assistance, spending in Massachusetts for health and hospitals exceeded the baseline in every year from 1979 to 1989. From 1979 through 1986, the gap was approximately constant between $60 and $70 per capita, as Massachusetts' spending tracked the growth of the benchmark; from 1986 onward the gap widened, reaching a spread of about $100 per capita, or about an 80 percent difference, by 1989. Throughout the period, Massachusetts showed a relatively high priority in this area of human services, with rising priority in the later years of the 1980s.

The Dispersion of Priorities

Over the course of the decade, Massachusetts' priority toward state spending in this area rose; in 1979 two states showed higher relative priority, while in 1989 only New York did. Figure 3-4 shows the distribution of states according to their actual spending in comparison to their individual benchmarks in 1989.

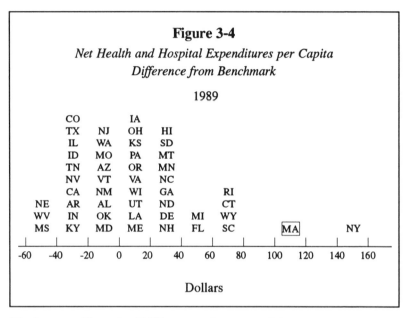

Figure 3-4

Net Health and Hospital Expenditures per Capita
Difference from Benchmark

1989

Understanding the Difference between Massachusetts and the National Average

Table 3-3 shows a reconciliation of Massachusetts' nominal 1989 net spending per capita on health and hospitals with the national average. The national average was about $130 per capita, while Massachusetts spent about $275. A favorable set of needs circumstances slightly reduced anticipated net state spending in Massachusetts, but this was offset by higher spending anticipated as a result of higher than average income. Input cost differences added approximately $20 per capita to the expected nominal benchmark, bringing it to about $160 per capita. Of the remaining difference, about $100 per capita was due to Massachusetts showing a higher priority than the benchmark, and the other approximately $15 reflected the higher input costs Massachusetts incurred as a result of its greater fiscal effort in this spending area.

Table 3-3

Reconciliation of National Average to Massachusetts Spending
Health and Hospitals Net State Spending per Capita, 1989

	Spending per capita (1989 dollars)	Percent of national average
National average spending		
Nominal national average	134	100
Adjustment to national average		
for Massachusetts input costs	18	13
Differences in circumstances		
Fiscal need indicators	-7	-5
Per capita income	11	8
Input costs associated with		
differences due to circumstances	1	0
Differences in choices		
Choice differences	104	77
Input costs associated with		
differences due to choices	14	10
Nominal Massachusetts 1989		
spending	275	204

Understanding the Change in Massachusetts' Health and Hospitals Spending, 1979–1989

Table 3-4 shows the components of the increase in Massachusetts' net spending on health and hospitals across the period. Massachusetts' real spending on health and hospitals rose by about $80 per capita, about 50 percent. A small change in Massachusetts' circumstances, national trends, and Massachusetts' rapid income increases together raised the expected spending level by about $35 per capita. The increase in the relative priority Massachusetts chose to display toward this spending area accounted for the remaining approximately $45 per capita increase. Thus, about 27 percentage points of the 47 percentage point increase resulted from a shift in the choice Massachusetts made about its spending priority in this area.

Table 3-4
Analysis of 1979–1989 Change in Real Massachusetts Spending
Health and Hospitals Net State Spending per Capita

	Spending per capita (1989 dollars)	Percent of 1979 spending
Massachusetts 1979 real spending	165	100
1979–1989 changes in circumstances		
Change in fiscal need indicators	4	2
Change in per capita income	23	14
General time trend and change in national choices	7	5
1979–1989 changes in choices	44	27
Massachusetts 1989 real spending	242	147

Commentary

Throughout the period from 1979 to 1989, Massachusetts spent considerably more in both major areas of human services programs than its anticipated benchmark, adjusted to reflect Massachusetts' different (and changing) circumstances. In both areas, Massachusetts began the period with somewhat higher spending than would be anticipated, and in both areas its relative emphasis diverged further from the benchmark over the period. This increasing divergence took place in spite of the fact that the benchmarks themselves increased substantially as a result of steady national spending growth and rapid income growth in Massachusetts.

Why did Massachusetts' priorities shift as they did? Part of the answer, at least for direct assistance, may lie in the changing pattern of federal funding. In 1979, federal support paid for 54 percent of direct assistance spending in Massachusetts; by 1989, it was providing only 46 percent. While Massachusetts increased its own real spending in this area by 55 percent, federal support increased by only 13 percent. Viewed from the perspective of recipients, total direct services spending per poor person (including federal funding) rose by only about 20 percent in real terms, while the inflation-adjusted state contribution per poor person rose about 40 percent. Massachusetts was able to provide an increasing level of real direct assistance benefits per poor person *in spite of* comparatively slow growth in the federal support of these programs—but only because the state was willing and able to make up the difference as the share of federal support declined.

CHAPTER FOUR

Highways

Across the nation, investment in highway infrastructure—in new building and in maintenance and operation of the existing infrastructure base—has become an area of increasing importance to the public officials who carry it out as much as to the commuters who drive on it, the businesses that ship their goods over it, and the taxpayers who pay for it. Aging facilities in the Northeast and rapidly expanding systems in the Southwest have created varying demands for infrastructure spending. This chapter examines the largest component of infrastructure spending by state and local governments: highways. Operating expenditures and total highway spending are each analyzed in turn; in both cases federal reimbursements to state and local governments are included, since state-by-state figures of federal transfers for transportation were not available.[1] Including federal funds allows an examination of the state's standing in terms of total investment in and maintenance of its highway infrastructure, an important factor in supporting the expansion of the economy.

Forming the Benchmark for Highways

The most obvious determinant of total highway spending is the size of the state's highway network. However, the number of miles of

---

1 Neither operating spending nor total spending is a perfect index of the level of services provided, which will depend both on current spending and on the history of highway construction and maintenance spending (the so-called "capital stock" of highway infrastructure). Unfortunately, there are no consistent and reliable data on the existing levels of past investment (net of depreciation), so current spending must be used instead.

highway already constructed is also a reflection of choices the state has made about how much emphasis to give to investments in infrastructure. As an alternative, the number of motor vehicles in the state was used as a measure of the need for highway spending.[2] Thus, the focus of the analysis was the amount of spending on highways *per motor vehicle* in the state. What factors should affect expenditures per vehicle? The number of vehicles per person may have an influence—when there are more cars per person, the state may not need to spend so much per car. The size of the state's highway system (miles of highway per motor vehicle) and the overall size of the state (geographic area per motor vehicle) may also influence the state's spending level. Climate affects the rate of road deterioration, and thus the need for spending on repairs; to allow for this effect, the number of "heating degree days" was included as an explanatory variable.[3] The degree of urbanization may also be an influence, so the percent of the population living in metropolitan areas was also included. As in the other analyses, income and a general time trend were included.[4]

Highway Operating Expenditures

Nominal spending in Massachusetts on highway operations closely approximated the national average throughout the 1980s. Nominal spending rose by more than 50 percent, from about $90 per motor vehicle in 1979 to about $140 in 1989. However, cost increases—both national and in Massachusetts in relation to the other states—would

---

2 Of course, the number of automobiles owned by people living in the state is also a choice that both influences and, possibly, reflects the choices they make about how much transportation infrastructure to invest in. However, the number of motor vehicles registered in a state may not always be an accurate reflection of the number actually operated on the state's highways—particularly in states with high insurance rates (like Massachusetts).

3 Appendix B describes how heating degree days are calculated.

4 Appendix C shows the regression results and detailed specifications of the variables used.

by themselves have caused spending to rise to about $170 per motor vehicle if the real level of spending had remained constant. Instead, the real level of highway operating services declined by about 20 percent.

Pattern of Massachusetts' Relative Priority over Time

Figure 4-1 shows the benchmark and actual operating spending on highways (in real 1989 dollars for all years) for Massachusetts for 1979 to 1989 based on the 49 sample states. The benchmark is relatively flat across the period, and its level is somewhat sensitive to how the estimating equation is specified; thus, we cannot be confident whether Massachusetts is above or below its benchmark. The *pattern* of change in comparison to the benchmark, however, is consistent across different estimates of the benchmark. While the

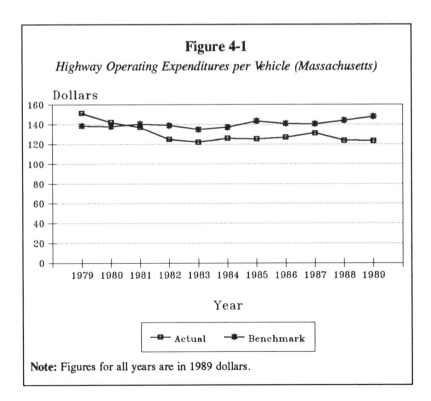

Figure 4-1

Highway Operating Expenditures per Vehicle (Massachusetts)

Note: Figures for all years are in 1989 dollars.

benchmark is approximately stable in real terms, Massachusetts' real spending declined substantially, falling about 20 percent between 1979 and 1983 and then remaining roughly constant through 1989. If, as the standard benchmark estimate shown in figure 4-1 suggests, Massachusetts was slightly above its benchmark in 1979, then it was below it by 1989. Measured against its estimated benchmark, Massachusetts spent about $15 per vehicle more than the benchmark in 1979, and about $25 less per motor vehicle in 1989. Massachusetts' relative spending priority toward highway operations was considerably lower in 1989 than at the start of the period.

The Dispersion of Priorities

Figure 4-2 charts the difference between each state's spending per motor vehicle on highways and its benchmark for 1989. In 1979, Massachusetts showed approximately the average emphasis on highway operations spending, standing 21st among the states in comparison to their standard benchmarks. By 1989, it had fallen to 41st.

Understanding the Difference between Massachusetts and the National Average

Table 4-1 shows a reconciliation of Massachusetts' nominal spending on highways in 1989 with the national average. Massachusetts faced considerably higher input costs, but actually spent $16 less per motor vehicle in nominal terms than the national average of $156. To match the national average (adjusting to reflect the Commonwealth's higher input costs), Massachusetts would have to spend about $175 per vehicle. The effects of its favorable circumstances and higher-than-average income net out to reduce anticipated spending to about $165 per vehicle. The choice Massachusetts has made in this area reduced its spending below the benchmark by about $25 per motor vehicle in nominal terms, about 15 percent.

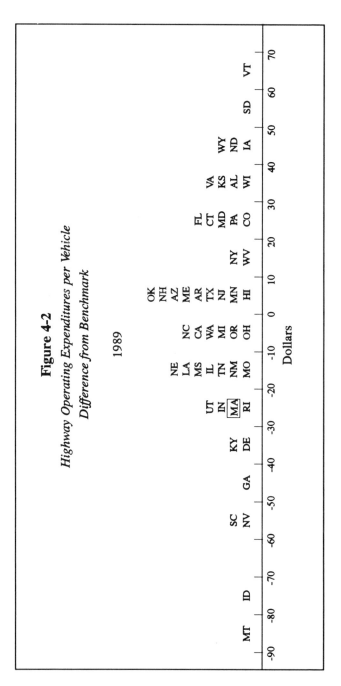

Figure 4-2

Highway Operating Expenditures per Vehicle
Difference from Benchmark

1989

Table 4-1
Reconciliation of National Average to Massachusetts Spending
Highway Operating Spending per Motor Vehicle, 1989

	Spending per motor vehicle (1989 dollars)	Percent of national average
National average spending		
Nominal national average	156	100
Adjustment to national average		
for Massachusetts input costs	21	13
Differences in circumstances		
Fiscal need indicators	-12	-7
Per capita income	3	2
Input costs associated with		
differences due to circumstances	-1	-1
Differences in choices		
Choice differences	-24	-16
Input costs associated with		
differences due to choices	-3	-2
Nominal Massachusetts 1989		
spending	140	90

Understanding the Change in Massachusetts' Highway Spending, 1979–1989

Table 4-2 shows the components of the change in highway spending in Massachusetts over the period from 1979 to 1989. Over this period, real spending on highway operations declined, on a per motor vehicle basis, by about 20 percent. Changes in fiscal circumstances and income approximately canceled each other out, while the general national trend raised anticipated spending in Massachusetts from its $150 per vehicle 1979 level to about $160 per vehicle. But Massachusetts lowered the priority it showed in this area by about $35 per motor vehicle in real terms, about 25 percent, across the decade, leaving its real spending at about $125 per vehicle by 1989.

Table 4-2

Analysis of 1979–1989 Change in Real Massachusetts Spending
Highway Operating Spending per Motor Vehicle

	Spending per motor vehicle (1989 dollars)	Percent of 1979 spending
Massachusetts 1979 real spending	151	100
1979–1989 changes in circumstances		
Change in fiscal need indicators	-6	-4
Change in per capita income	7	4
General time trend and changes in national choices	8	5
1979–1989 changes in choices	-37	-25
Massachusetts 1989 real spending	123	81

Total Highway Spending (including capital)

While operating spending on highways decreased in real terms across the decade, *total* highway spending (including capital expenditures) rose slightly in real terms. In *nominal* terms, total highway spending expanded briskly later in the decade, nearly doubling between 1984 and 1989 after growing slowly between 1979 and 1984. Nominal spending rose from about $150 per motor vehicle in 1979 to about $290 per motor vehicle in 1989. Of the approximately $140 per motor vehicle increase, $130 would have been required to maintain spending at the same level in real terms as national inflation (and some additional increases in Massachusetts prices) pushed costs up. Only about $10 of the increase per motor vehicle is attributable to an expansion of spending in real terms.

Throughout the period, Massachusetts' nominal total spending on highways was well below (about $50 per vehicle) the national average. In 1979, Massachusetts ranked 41st among the states in nominal total highway spending per motor vehicle; by 1989 it had risen to 35th.

Pattern of Massachusetts' Relative Priority over Time

Figure 4-3 shows benchmark and actual total spending on highways (in real 1989 dollars for each year) across the study period. Total highway expenditures increased by only about 3 percent in real terms, as real spending fell through 1984 and gradually recovered over the latter part of the 1980s. Since real operating spending fell about 20 percent over the period, this implies that capital spending rose in real terms. Throughout the period, total highway capital and operating expenditures per motor vehicle were well below what would be

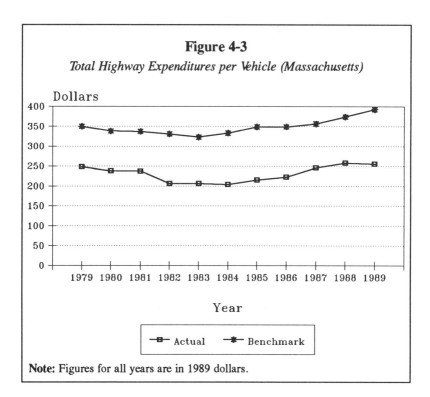

Figure 4-3

Total Highway Expenditures per Vehicle (Massachusetts)

Note: Figures for all years are in 1989 dollars.

expected based on Massachusetts' circumstances and other states' values. Over the decade, the gap between actual and benchmark spending in Massachusetts increased from about $100 to about $140 per motor vehicle.

The Dispersion of Priorities

Figure 4-4 is a chart of states distributed by their actual total highway spending in comparison to their benchmarks for 1989. Massachusetts stood below all but two other states in this measure of overall priority shown toward highway spending. Its priority for combined capital and operating spending was even lower than its priority toward operating spending alone.

Understanding the Difference between Massachusetts and the National Average

Table 4-3 shows a reconciliation of Massachusetts' nominal spending on highway operations and capital investments combined in 1989 with the national average. If Massachusetts had spent at the national average rate (adjusted for higher Massachusetts input costs), it would have had to spend about half again more than it spent in 1989. The effect of fiscal circumstances and higher income roughly canceled each other. Therefore, the difference between Massachusetts' and national average spending in this area was due to Massachusetts' choices—about $140 per car (about one-third) less than would be expected on the basis of its benchmark.

Understanding the Change in Massachusetts' Highway Spending, 1979–1989

Table 4-4 shows the components of change in Massachusetts' total highway spending over the decade. Real spending on highway capital investments and operations combined rose by only about 3 percent from 1979 to 1989. Over the same period, per capita income—and state revenues—rose dramatically. Based on the relationship between

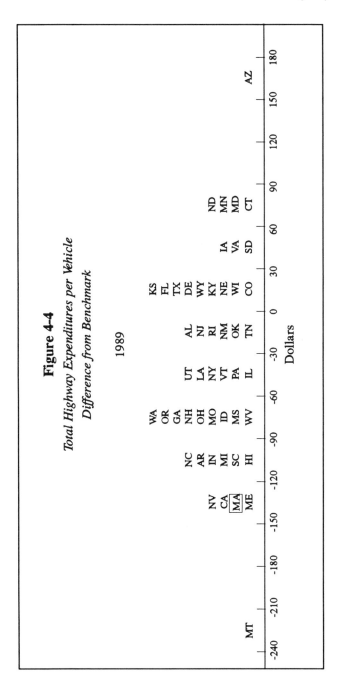

Figure 4-4

Total Highway Expenditures per Vehicle
Difference from Benchmark

1989

Table 4-3

Reconciliation of National Average to Massachusetts Spending
Total Highway Spending per Motor Vehicle, 1989

	Spending per motor vehicle (1989 dollars)	Percent of national average
National average spending		
Nominal national average	391	100
Adjustment to national average		
for Massachusetts input costs	55	14
Differences in circumstances		
Fiscal need indicators	-16	-4
Per capita income	18	5
Input costs associated with		
differences due to circumstances	0	0
Differences in choices		
Choice differences	-137	-35
Input costs associated with		
differences due to choices	-19	-5
Nominal Massachusetts 1989		
spending	291	74

income and highway spending observed in other states, Massachusetts' income growth alone would have been expected to add spending of about $35 per vehicle over the period, while the general national trend would have increased Massachusetts' spending by about $15 per car. The combined impact of these factors, together with a small favorable shift in fiscal circumstances, would have been to raise anticipated spending, holding Massachusetts' 1979 priority constant, to about $290 per car. Instead, the priority Massachusetts exhibited to total highway spending fell by about $35 per car, about 15 percent of 1979 spending, across the period, leaving 1989 real spending at about $255 per vehicle, nearly identical to real spending in 1979.

Table 4-4

Analysis of 1979–1989 Change in Real Massachusetts Spending
Total Highway Spending per Motor Vehicle

	Spending per motor vehicle (1989 dollars)	Percent of 1979 spending
Massachusetts 1979 real spending	248	100
1979–1989 changes in circumstances		
Change in fiscal need indicators	-9	-4
Change in per capita income	36	15
General time trend and changes in national choices	16	6
1979–1989 changes in choices	-36	-14
Massachusetts 1989 real spending	255	103

Commentary

In spite of strong income growth that would be anticipated to spur increased spending on highways, real spending on highway operations declined by about 20 percent in Massachusetts on a per motor vehicle basis from 1979 to 1989. This reflects a considerable reduction in the relative priority given to this component of spending. Massachusetts moved from being, in 1979, above the middle—21st—in the national distribution of states in terms of the relative priority accorded to highway operating spending to a spending priority rank of 41st in 1989. The decline in operating spending relative to the benchmark over the period was offset by an increase in capital spending, as total spending remained nearly constant in real terms. In the latter part of the 1980s, total spending closely paralleled the benchmark—but at a level about one-third below anticipated spending. The gap between actual and benchmark total spending was about $140 per car in 1989, while the gap in operating highway spending was only about $25 per vehicle. Thus, a large fraction of the gap in total spending reflects a relatively low rate of capital expenditures per vehicle (as compared with other states). While the priority shown toward capital spending rose somewhat over the course of the decade, it remained well below that shown by other states on average. This may reflect the fact that Massachusetts is a mature state in terms of its infrastructure, with most of its major highways already built. It may also reflect a choice to emphasize public mass transit rather than highways as a transportation strategy; over the course of the 1980s, Massachusetts' state government significantly increased its investments in mass transit. On the other hand, it may reflect a low level of recapitalization as the general highway infrastructure ages.

In Massachusetts, financing of highway expenditures is split roughly 55–45 between the state and local levels. Overall, this mix of support resulted in a small decline in emphasis over the decade. But the *operating* component—where local government plays a larger role—showed a substantial decline in priority, while the *capital* component—where the state plays the larger role—showed an increase. Once again, this pattern seems to reflect the relative availablity of funds at the two levels of government during the 1980s.

CHAPTER FIVE

Public Safety and Corrections

Spending on public safety[1] (which includes police, crime prevention and detection, and fire fighting and prevention activities) and on corrections together constitute about 9 percent of combined state and local spending.[2] Expenditures in these areas rose significantly across the nation over the course of the 1980s, and are an increasing source of pressure on both state and local budgets. Public safety is almost exclusively a local responsibility; in Massachusetts, 88 percent of expenditures for public safety are by local government units. Corrections, by contrast, is principally a state activity; in Massachusetts, 83 percent of expenditures are by state government.

Forming the Benchmarks for Public Safety and Corrections

For both public safety and corrections expenditures, the principal determinant of the required level of spending is likely to be the size of the state's population. Thus, the appropriate focus for analysis in these areas is spending per capita. What other state characteristics (in addition to population size) should be expected to drive spending? The most obvious is the crime rate; since crime is often concentrated

---

1   The Census data on state and local expenditures used in this study treat corrections as a subcategory of public safety. In this study, the two are treated independently. Thus, public safety will refer to public safety expenditures *excluding* corrections expenditures.

2   Capital as well as operating costs were included in both public safety and corrections, as the data were not available over the entire study period to separate out capital costs.

in poorer communities, the poverty rate was also included. Because the cost of providing these services may be influenced by a community's degree of urbanization, the percentage of the population living in metropolitan areas was also included. As in all the analyses, income and a general time trend were included.[3]

Public Safety (excluding Corrections)

Nominal public safety expenditures in Massachusetts nearly doubled from 1979 to 1989, rising from about $120 per capita to nearly $240 per capita. By the end of 1989, nominal spending had risen to about $80 per capita more than in the average state. The number of per capita dollars spent in the Commonwealth was substantially greater than the national average throughout the 1980s. Massachusetts ranks very high in comparison to other states; in 1979 it ranked 3d and in 1989 it ranked 4th in comparison to other states' nominal spending.

Nominal spending doubled, but essentially all of the increase was attributable to the increasing cost of providing the same level of services. National inflation accounted for about $90 of the increase, while the increase of prices in Massachusetts relative to the rest of the nation would have added about another $30 to the cost if there had been no change in the level of services provided. In fact, the real level of services declined by about 1 percent.

Pattern of Massachusetts' Relative Priority over Time

Figure 5-1 shows the benchmark and actual public safety spending (in real 1989 dollars for all years) for Massachusetts for 1979 to 1989 based on the 49 sample states. Massachusetts' spending in this area was substantially higher than the benchmark in 1979. A major change occurred at the beginning of the period, when, over the course of

---

3   Appendix C shows the detailed specification of the variables used and presents the regression results.

three years, real spending on public safety in Massachusetts declined by about 20 percent. By 1982, the Commonwealth's spending was almost exactly equal to the benchmark. Spending tracked the benchmark closely for the balance of the decade. The net effect of the spending drop early in the decade and the gradual rise since 1982 was a fall, overall, of about 1 percent in real spending on public safety.

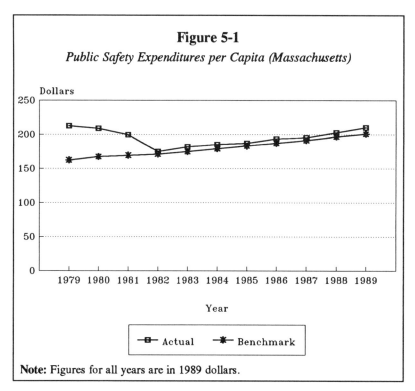

Figure 5-1

Public Safety Expenditures per Capita (Massachusetts)

Note: Figures for all years are in 1989 dollars.

Understanding the Change in Massachusetts' Public Safety Spending, 1979–1989

Table 5-1 shows the components of the change in public safety spending in Massachusetts over the period from 1979 to 1989. Real spending fell by about 1 percent, from $213 per capita to about $210 per capita, over the period. To maintain a constant priority, however, the Commonwealth would have had to increase real spending by about

20 percent instead of maintaining real spending at a steady level. The substantial rise in per capita income in the Commonwealth over the period would have been expected to raise the real public safety spending by about $20 per capita; a strong national trend of increased spending in this area, if followed by Massachusetts, would have raised real spending by another $25 per capita. These two increases were offset slightly by a small favorable shift in the state's public safety circumstances, but together these forces could have been expected to raise spending to about $250 per capita if the state had maintained the same level of relative priority toward spending in this area. Instead, the state's priority shifted down by about $40 per capita, about 20 percent, leaving the real level of spending in 1989 virtually unchanged from its 1979 level.

The story of the change in public safety spending in Massachusetts has two major parts. First, there was a substantial nationwide increase in real spending in this area. Second, Massachusetts significantly reduced its real spending from 1979 to 1982, moving from a very

Table 5-1

Analysis of 1979–1989 Change in Real Massachusetts Spending
Public Safety Spending per Capita

	Spending per capita (1989 dollars)	Percent of 1979 spending
Massachusetts 1979 real spending	213	100
1979–1989 changes in circumstances		
Change in fiscal need indicators	-6	-3
Change in per capita income	19	9
General time trend and change in national choices	26	12
1979–1989 changes in choices	-41	-19
Massachusetts 1989 real spending	210	99

high relative priority to being more typical in comparison to other states. For the remainder of the decade, Massachusetts joined the national trend. These two components almost exactly offset each other, leaving real spending virtually unchanged.

Understanding the Difference between Massachusetts and the National Average

Table 5-2 shows a reconciliation of Massachusetts' actual nominal spending on public safety in 1989 with the national average. In 1989, Massachusetts spent about $50, about 30 percent, more per capita than the national average of $185. About half of the difference is attributable to the higher input costs Massachusetts faces. Nearly another third of the difference is attributable to having higher income and slightly less favorable circumstances than the national average. Only about 5 percentage points of the roughly 30 percentage point difference is a result of Massachusetts exhibiting a higher priority in this area than is observed in the average state.

The Dispersion of Priorities

Figure 5-2 charts the difference between each state's spending on public safety and its benchmark for 1989. Massachusetts stands slightly higher than the bulk of other states, with only 8 states showing a higher relative priority. Its difference in relative effort compared to the large block of other states showing lower priority, however, is relatively small (about $10 to $20 per capita). Thus, while Massachusetts' rank is high in the national distribution, there is little difference among the middle 30 or so states in this measure of relative effort in public safety spending.

Corrections

Both in nominal and in real terms, corrections spending was one of the fastest-growing components of state and local spending in the nation over the course of the 1980s, and Massachusetts was no

Table 5-2

Reconciliation of National Average to Massachusetts Spending
Public Safety Spending (excluding Corrections) per Capita
1989

	Spending per capita (1989 dollars)	Percent of national average
National average spending		
Nominal national average	185	100
Adjustment to national average		
for Massachusetts input costs	24	13
Differences in circumstances		
Fiscal need indicators	7	4
Per capita income	9	5
Input costs associated with		
differences due to circumstances	2	1
Differences in choices		
Choice differences	9	5
Input costs associated with		
differences due to choices	1	1
Nominal Massachusetts 1989		
spending	238	129

exception. From 1979 to 1989, nominal spending on corrections in Massachusetts very nearly quadrupled, rising from just over $22 per capita in 1979 to nearly $88 per capita in 1989. The cost of providing the 1979 level of services roughly doubled over the period; three quarters of that change was due to national inflation, while the other one quarter was accounted for by the increase in prices in Massachusetts relative to those in the nation as a whole. But real spending also increased by about $40 per capita, an amount almost double what was paid for the level of services provided in 1979. Throughout the period,

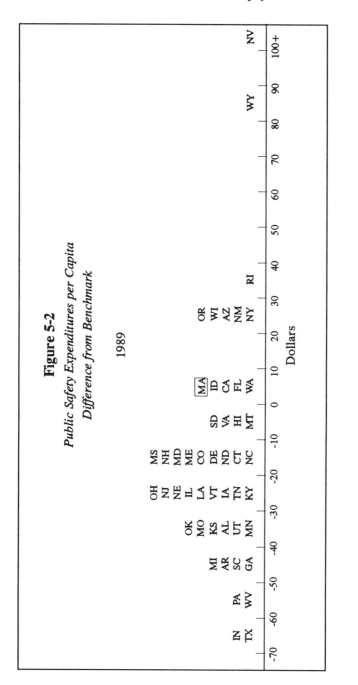

Figure 5-2

Public Safety Expenditures per Capita
Difference from Benchmark

1989

Massachusetts' nominal spending closely tracked the national average, rising slightly above the average of other states in 1988 and 1989.

Understanding the Difference between Massachusetts and the National Average

Nominal spending figures mask the relatively low priority Massachusetts placed on corrections spending. Table 5-3 shows a reconciliation of Massachusetts' nominal 1989 spending per capita on corrections with the national average. Massachusetts spent about $15 more per capita than the national average of about $75 in 1989; most of the difference, about $10 per capita, lies in the higher input

Table 5-3

Reconciliation of National Average to Massachusetts Spending Corrections Spending per Capita, 1989

	Spending per capita (1989 dollars)	Percent of national average
National average spending		
Nominal national average	75	100
Adjustment to national average for Massachusetts input costs	10	13
Differences in circumstances		
Fiscal need indicators	-1	1
Per capita income	9	11
Input costs associated with differences due to circumstances	1	1
Differences in choices		
Choice differences	-6	7
Input costs associated with differences due to choices	-1	1
Nominal Massachusetts 1989 spending	88	116

costs it faces. The fact that Massachusetts has higher than average per capita income raises anticipated spending roughly an additional $10 per capita. This is offset by the fact that Massachusetts shows somewhat less than the average priority toward spending in this area; the Commonwealth spent between 5 and 10 percent less in this area than would be expected for the average state if it faced the same circumstances.

Pattern of Massachusetts' Relative Priority over Time

Figure 5-3 shows the benchmark and actual spending (both in real 1989 dollars for all years) for Massachusetts for 1979 to 1989 based on the 49 sample states. Actual spending in Massachusetts lies below the benchmark in every year of the period. Massachusetts began the period spending about 15 percent less than would have been expected

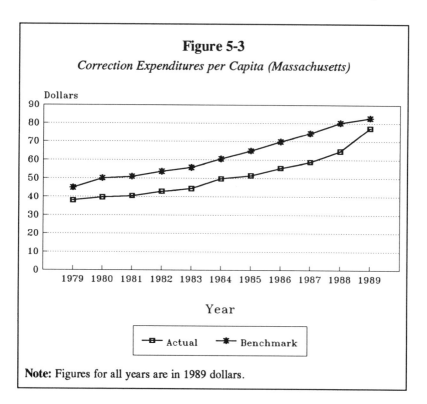

Figure 5-3

Correction Expenditures per Capita (Massachusetts)

Note: Figures for all years are in 1989 dollars.

based on its circumstances. Between 1980 and 1988, the gap between benchmark and actual spending grew slowly, from about $10 to about $15 per capita. In 1989, however, a relatively abrupt increase in actual spending reduced the gap substantially to about $6 per capita, about 8 percent of the 1989 benchmark.

The Dispersion of Priorities

Figure 5-4 shows the distribution of states according to their actual spending in comparison to their individual benchmarks in 1989. Massachusetts is slightly below the center of the national distribution in terms of the relative priority shown toward corrections, ranking 27th among the states in 1989 (up from 32d in 1979).

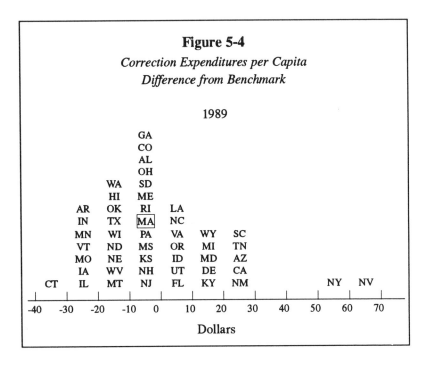

Figure 5-4

Correction Expenditures per Capita
Difference from Benchmark

Table 5-4

Analysis of 1979–1989 Change in Real Massachusetts Spending
Corrections Spending per Capita

	Spending per capita (1989 dollars)	Percent of 1979 spending
Massachusetts 1979 real spending	38	100
1979–1989 changes in circumstances		
Change in fiscal need indicators	-6	-15
Change in per capita income	18	46
General time trend and changes in national choices	26	67
1979–1989 changes in choices	1	3
Massachusetts 1989 real spending	77	203

Understanding the Change in Massachusetts' Corrections Spending, 1979–1989

Table 5-4 shows the components of the increase in Massachusetts' spending on corrections across the period. Real spending on corrections in Massachusetts almost exactly doubled over the period, rising from just under $40 per capita to just under $80 per capita. The increase is almost completely accounted for by the general national trends and the increase in per capita income in Massachusetts. About $25 of the increase, about two-thirds of the total, is accounted for by the general time trend and changes in national choices, and nearly $20 by the increase in real incomes in Massachusetts over the period. A favorable shift in needs indicators in this area reduced anticipated spending by about $6 per capita. The priority given to this area by the Commonwealth was essentially stable across the period.

Commentary

Combined spending in Massachusetts on public safety and corrections closely approximated expected benchmark spending in 1989, having fallen from a level considerably above the benchmark in 1979. Public safety spending experienced a sharp decline in relative priority, falling by about 20 percent in real terms and relative to the benchmark, between 1979 and 1982. It tracked the benchmark's rise for the remainder of the period, but still closed the decade with slightly lower real spending than it had in 1979, and with a considerably lower relative priority than it had then enjoyed. Corrections spending began the period somewhat below the benchmark, and generally tracked the rising growth anticipated as a result of the national trend and rising income in the state. In 1988, an upward shift in relative priority for this area substantially closed the gap between benchmark and actual spending. Over the period, spending in both areas moved toward the benchmark—the priority on public safety decreasing and on corrections increasing—and by 1989 was very close to what would be anticipated on the basis of the expenditures made by other states.

It is worth noting that the area of public protection spending in which Massachusetts' relative priority was stable or rising across the period—corrections—is about 85 percent financed through the state government, while about 90 percent of the financing for the area in which the relative priority declined—public safety other than corrections—is through the local level of government. While the rapid expansion of revenues at the state level permitted nominal corrections expenditures in the state to quadruple, and real expenditures to double, keeping up with a rapidly rising benchmark, public safety expenditures on police, fire, and other largely locally financed public protection programs closed the period at the same real level at which they began it.

The largest components of the changes over the decade were a strong national real spending trend and rapidly rising input costs. Together, they caused a swelling of nominal spending nationwide that can easily obscure the more subtle but quite significant shifts in the priority shown toward public safety spending. When the changes in priority are separated from other factors, a clear pattern emerges: the emphasis on locally financed programs declined, while the priority accorded to state-financed programs increased. And since Massachusetts started the period showing very high priority toward locally financed public safety programs, and low priority toward state-funded corrections programs, its value choices in this area became more like those of other states over the period.

CHAPTER SIX

Total General Expenditures

Examining the total spending—referred to in the Census data as the "general expenditures"—of a state, its associated authorities, and all its towns and municipalities provides a comprehensive view of the state's public service provision. This chapter looks at general expenditures, including all major areas of spending, for current services as well as for capital projects. A significant component of each state's spending comes from the federal government; about 15 percent of Massachusetts' spending is currently reimbursed, in one way or another, by federal programs. The state's general expenditures therefore can be examined either on a gross basis (including spending backed by federal funds) or on a net basis (removing any federally reimbursed spending). As the principal purpose of this study is to examine the priorities embedded in how Massachusetts spends its own funds, the focus in this chapter will be on general expenditures *net of federal reimbursement*.[1]

In nominal terms, net public spending in the Commonwealth expanded markedly from 1979 to 1989, more than doubling from about $1500 to about $3300 per capita. About 70 percentage points of the approximately 120 percent increase, about three-fifths of the total, can be attributed to the rising cost of providing the same real level of services as nationwide inflation pushed up input costs. An additional 20 percentage points (about one-sixth of the total) can be

---

1   Net general expenditures were constructed from total general expenditures by subtracting: federal transfers to state and local governments for direct assistance, elementary and secondary education, and higher education.

attributed to the fact that Massachusetts experienced more rapid inflation than the rest of the country. About $400 per capita, however, about one-fourth of the total increase, represents an increase in the real level of services financed by state and local governments in the Commonwealth. Real public services funded by Massachusetts state and local governments expanded by about 15 percent.

Throughout the period, Massachusetts' net in-state-financed general expenditures exceeded those of the average state on a nominal, per capita basis. From 1979 through 1985, Massachusetts' spending was only slightly higher than the average. Beginning in 1986, nominal spending in the Commonwealth began to diverge increasingly from the average of other states. By 1989, Massachusetts was spending about $600 per capita (about 25 percent of the national average) more out of its own funds than the average state. Massachusetts ranked 7th among the states in general public expenditures.

Forming the Benchmark

Explanatory variables that drive all major components of public spending can be expected to influence the pattern of general expenditures observed across the states. Education and human services are the two largest components of this spending in most states; thus, the size of the school-age population, the poverty rate in the state, and the proportion of elderly people in the population would be expected to be important explanatory variables. In addition, the fraction of the state's population living in metropolitan areas may be expected to influence the cost of many public programs. Many other variables could be included, and might make some difference in the precise level of the benchmark estimates. Generally, the *pattern* of the benchmark across time is affected relatively little by changes in the explanatory variables included, but the *level* tends to vary somewhat.[2]

---

2 Appendix C shows the precise specification of the explanatory variables included in the general expenditures benchmark estimation and provides the regression results.

Pattern of Massachusetts' Relative Priority over Time

Figure 6-1 shows the benchmark and actual general expenditures net of federal reimbursements (both in real 1989 dollars for all years) for Massachusetts for 1979 to 1989 based on the 49 sample states. The estimated level of this benchmark is somewhat sensitive to the specification of the estimating equation, with some estimates showing the benchmark somewhat lower than the standard benchmark shown in Figure 6-1. The pattern of changes between actual and benchmark spending is quite similar across different estimates of the benchmark, however, and, if anything, the alternative estimates suggest that Massachusetts' net public spending exceeds the benchmark by more than Figure 6-1 would suggest.

Figure 6-1 shows that Massachusetts' overall net state public spending was noticeably higher than would be anticipated on the basis of the priorities exhibited by other states. At the beginning of the

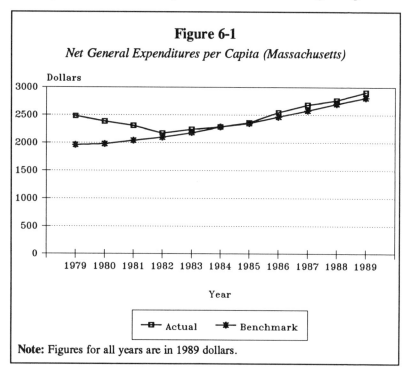

Figure 6-1

Net General Expenditures per Capita (Massachusetts)

Note: Figures for all years are in 1989 dollars.

period, the Commonwealth's spending exceeded the benchmark based on the state's then-current circumstances by over $500 per capita, about 25 percent. From 1979 through 1982, real per capita spending declined by about $300 per capita (about 12 percent). At the same time, expected benchmark spending rose by over $150 per capita, leaving the Commonwealth's spending only a little above the benchmark. From 1982 through 1989, benchmark spending increased slightly more rapidly than actual spending; by 1989, the difference between benchmark and actual spending was only about $100 per capita, about 3 percent. Over the course of the decade, Massachusetts appears to have experienced a downward shift in its overall emphasis on public spending; from a point well above the benchmark in 1979, its spending was, by 1989, nearly indistinguishable from what would be expected on the basis of other states.

The gap between Massachusetts' actual spending and its benchmark is greater when general *operating* expenditures are considered;[3] in 1989, Massachusetts spent over $300 per capita in excess of its benchmark for general operating expenditures (including federal reimbursements). This suggests that Massachusetts has a higher relative priority for operating spending, in comparison to other states, than for capital spending.

The Dispersion of Priorities

Figure 6-2 shows the 49 sample states distributed according to the gap between their actual spending and their individually computed benchmarks in 1989. In 1979, Massachusetts exhibited one of the highest priorities for overall public services (where each state is compared to its individual benchmark), spending over $500 per capita more out of its own funds than would be expected based on the behavior of other states. The Commonwealth ranked second only to New York in its relative willingness to support general services out

---

3 General operating expenditures do not include spending on capital projects.

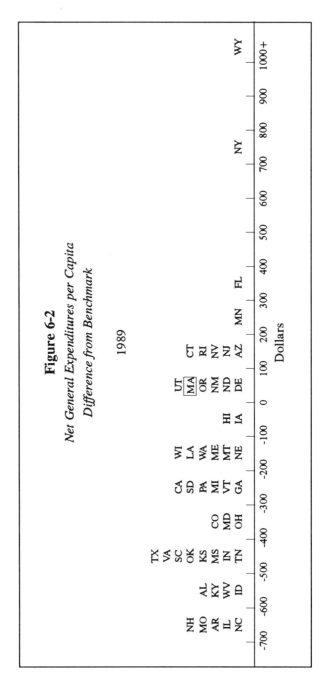

Figure 6-2

Net General Expenditures per Capita

Difference from Benchmark

1989

of its own funds. The rapidly decreasing priority Massachusetts accorded to in-state-funded public services in the early 1980s, however, led Massachusetts to be only a little higher than its benchmark in 1989, and therefore much more typical in comparison to other states. Spending of about $100 per capita more than its benchmark for public services made Massachusetts the 11th-ranked state in 1989, with spending only a little higher than that of the approximately 20 states that make up the middle of the national distribution. Over the course of the 1980s, Massachusetts went from having one of the highest propensities in the nation to fund public services out of in-state funds to being much more like most other states.

Understanding the Difference between Massachusetts and the National Average

In 1989, Massachusetts spent about 10 percent more per capita than the average state for self-financed general expenditures. Its relatively favorable fiscal needs circumstances would suggest lower spending than in other states, but a combination of its higher input costs, higher than average per capita income, and a somewhat higher than average propensity to support general public services out of in-state funds more than offset its favorable circumstances. Table 6-1 shows a reconciliation of the national average to the nominal spending in Massachusetts in 1989. National average spending was about $3000 per capita in 1989; Massachusetts' nominal spending exceeded this by about $300 per capita, about 10 percent. Favorable fiscal needs indicators (as compared to other states) reduced the need for spending in Massachusetts (judging from the behavior of other states) by about $300 per capita. Substantially higher per capita income than the average state increased anticipated spending in Massachusetts by about $130 per capita. Higher input costs contributed about $380 per capita to Massachusetts' spending. The remaining $110 nominal difference is due to the higher relative priority Massachusetts chose

Table 6-1

Reconciliation of National Average to Massachusetts Spending
General Expenditures Net of Federal Reimbursements per Capita, 1989

	Per capita spending (1989 dollars)	Percent of national average
National average spending		
Nominal national average	2985	100
Adjustment to national average for Massachusetts input costs	407	14
Differences in circumstances		
Fiscal need indicators	-301	-10
Per capita income	129	4
Input costs associated with differences due to circumstances	-24	-1
Differences in choices		
Choice differences	97	3
Input costs associated with differences due to choices	13	0
Nominal Massachusetts 1989 spending	3305	111

to give to overall public services, along with the extra input costs required to produce that higher level of services.

Understanding the Change in Massachusetts' Spending, 1979–1989

What accounted for the changes in Massachusetts' spending over the decade? Table 6-2 shows the changes in real terms, separated into components of changes in circumstances and in choices. Real spending on in-state-funded public services provided by government rose from about $2500 to about $2900 per capita, by about 15 percent,

Table 6-2

Decomposition of 1979–1989 Change in Real Massachusetts Spending General Expenditures Net of Federal Reimbursements per Capita

	Per capita spending (1989 dollars)	Percent of 1979 spending
Massachusetts 1979 real spending	2481	100
1979–1989 changes in circumstances		
Change in fiscal need indicators	120	5
Change in per capita income	266	11
General time trend	468	19
1979–1989 changes in choices	-425	-17
Massachusetts 1989 real spending	2909	117

over the period from 1979 to 1989. Increased spending of $120 per capita was expected as a result of changes in Massachusetts' fiscal needs circumstances, another $265 per capita as a result of the substantial increase in per capita income in the state, and of an additional $465 per capita as a result of the observed national trend in general operating spending. If Massachusetts had not changed the relative priority it showed toward this area of spending, its real spending would have increased by about 35 percent, to about $3,350 per capita by 1989. Instead, Massachusetts shifted the relatively high priority it showed in 1979, reducing expenditures by about $425 per capita. This cut the 1979 disparity between actual and anticipated spending by four-fifths, leaving Massachusetts only about $100 per capita in excess of its benchmark.

Commentary

In 1979, Massachusetts exhibited a noticeably high relative priority for in-state-funded public services. In real terms, in-state-supported general spending then declined by about 12 percent between 1979 and 1982. Several forces probably combined to reduce overall spending relative to the benchmark. First, Proposition 2½ both directly imposed restrictions on spending at the local level and put officials on notice that the public seemed to want spending cuts. Second, the national economy was going through a recessionary period. Finally, a relatively conservative Democratic administration controlled the Massachusetts state executive offices.

From 1982 onward, Massachusetts' state-supported general expenditures rose at roughly the pace set by the benchmark. Nationwide, government spending grew rapidly, and the increasing state revenues in Massachusetts permitted it to keep pace with the rapidly rising benchmark—in spite of the restrictions on local spending embodied in Proposition 2½. The pattern outlined in Figure 6-1 appears to reflect the implementation of Proposition 2½ at the beginning of the decade and the period of rapid state revenue growth fueled by the rise in personal income in the latter part of the decade.

CHAPTER SEVEN

Massachusetts' Spending Priorities: By Choice or By Chance?

State and local spending in Massachusetts was transformed over the course of the 1980s. Total public spending grew rapidly, rising by 25 percent in real terms, but its component parts grew at radically different rates. After adjustment for inflation, federally supported spending declined by 25 percent, local government expenditures were constant and state government expenditures rose by 61 percent. The state government became more important, and local governments less—indeed, local government spending would have fallen by approximately 10 percent in real terms had not the state significantly increased its transfers to cities and towns.

Along the way, the value choices inherent in Massachusetts' spending decisions were profoundly altered. The Commonwealth's governments collectively lowered the overall priority exhibited toward public spending. As a result of rapidly rising income in the state and the strong growth trend observed across the nation, spending in Massachusetts could have been expected to increase more than it actually did across the period. Massachusetts began the period showing an exceptionally high level of spending in comparison to what might be expected on the basis of other states, and if the Commonwealth had maintained the same level of priority, total state and local spending supported by in-state funds would have been expected to be about $2.5 billion, about 15 percent, higher than it actually was in 1989. Ranked against other states in terms of in-state-financed general expenditures by state and local governments, Massachusetts fell from 2d in 1979 to 11th in 1989.

As the overall emphasis on public spending declined, the change was felt unevenly across different spending areas—the pattern of spending was transformed more profoundly than the level of spending. Table 7-1 summarizes the changes in Massachusetts' spending priorities from 1979 to 1989, showing how the gap between actual and benchmark spending shifted (in real dollars and as a percentage of the 1989 benchmark) and how the state's rank in terms of relative effort compared to other states changed.

By far the most significant shift was in elementary and secondary education, where the choices component of state spending fell by about $1100 per student. If the state had maintained the (very high) level of priority it accorded to K–12 public education in 1979, its 1989 spending would have been about 25 percent higher than it actually was. In comparison to other states, the priority shown by Massachusetts (measured by the gap between its actual and its benchmark spending) declined markedly; Massachusetts moved from being first in the nation in 1979 to being 21st in 1989.

By contrast, the relative priority shown toward public higher education increased (though not dramatically), with spending per student rising about $550 more than the benchmark did across the period. Compared to other states, Massachusetts raised the relative priority it showed toward spending on higher education; measured by the gap between actual and benchmark spending, its rank rose by 7 from 48th to 41st.

The priority shown toward human services also increased over the course of the period. Spending out of in-state funds for direct assistance rose by about $350 per poor person more than would have been anticipated on the basis of national trends and changes in Massachusetts' circumstances; if Massachusetts had maintained the priority it showed in 1979, its spending would have been about 20 percent lower in 1989 than it actually was. Similarly, Massachusetts increased the amount by which its spending on health and hospitals,

Table 7-1
Changes in Differences between Actual and Benchmark Spending
Massachusetts, 1979–1989[a]

	Change in Actual vs. Benchmark ($)[b]	Percent[c]	Change in Rank
General Expenditures financed in state	-425 per capita	-15	fell 9
Education			
Elementary and secondary	-1111 per student	-24	fell 20
Higher education	+530 per student	+6	rose 7
Human Services			
Direct assistance	+351 per poor person	+19	no change
Health and hospitals	+44 per capita	+32	rose 1
Highways			
Operations	-37 per motor vehicle	-25	fell 20
Total (including capital)	-36 per motor vehicle	-9	fell 6
Public Safety and Corrections			
Public Safety	-41 per capita	-20	fell 7
Corrections	+1 per capita	+1	rose 5

[a] All dollar figures are adjusted for inflation and to remove state-to-state variations in input costs, and are expressed in real 1989 dollars.

[b] Change, from 1979 to 1989, in the difference between actual and benchmark spending, in units as shown. For example, +100 in this column indicates that the amount by which the state's spending exceeds the benchmark increased by an additional $100 over the course of the period from 1979 to 1989.

[c] The 1979 to 1989 change in actual versus benchmark spending as a percent of 1989 benchmark spending.

net of charges, exceeded its benchmark. Over the course of the period the choices component of this area of spending rose by about $45 per capita. If the 1979 level of priority had remained in place through the period, 1989 spending would have been about 30 percent lower than it actually was.

The priority shown toward highway spending—both on operations and overall—decreased. The choices component of both operations and total spending fell by about $35 per motor vehicle, reducing operations spending by about 25 percent of what it would have been expected to be if the level of priority shown in 1979 had remained fixed. Its rank among states in terms of relative priority shown toward highway operations spending fell by 20 (from 21st to 41st), and toward total highway spending by 6 (from 41st to 47th).

The priority shown toward public safety also shifted downward across the decade, particularly in the early 1980s, when real spending declined by 20 percent over the course of three years. If the priority exhibited toward public safety had remained fixed across the decade at the 1979 level, 1989 spending would have been about 20 percent higher than it turned out to be; compared to other states, its rank fell by 7 on this measure of relative valuation placed on public spending (from 2d to 9th). By contrast, the priority shown toward corrections remained essentially unchanged (although Massachusetts' rank actually rose by 5, from 32d to 27th, since many other states showed declines in priority in this area).

Why did Massachusetts' Value Choices Change?

Over the course of the decade from 1979 to 1989 priorities in different spending areas shifted in patterns that were markedly different from each other and from the national average. The priority shown toward investment in elementary and secondary education, public safety spending, and in maintaining and operating the Commonwealth's highway system declined, and in the case of education and highways that drop was substantial. By contrast, the emphasis on higher education and on human services increased.

One agent of change in the state was the rapid rise in real incomes. The effects of changing income were incorporated when the benchmarks were constructed. Thus, the change in spending in comparison to the benchmark was not driven by income shifts. To explain the shifts, we must look *beyond* the income shifts and other changes in the circumstances that drive spending (for example, changes in the number of schoolchildren). Actual spending changed *relative to* benchmarks that incorporated the important identified influences.

There are two possible explanations. Perhaps the people of Massachusetts changed their minds. Perhaps they decided they did not like the values embodied in spending as it was carried out in 1979, and saw to it that changes were made. The groundswell of popular support for Proposition 2½—which experts widely predicted would fail—may have been a product of just such an explicit judgment about what values the people of the Commonwealth wanted reflected in the spending conducted on their behalf.

On the other hand, it may be that not all of the shifts were generated by a conscious change of heart on the part of voters. The areas of significant expansion in relative priority—higher education, direct assistance, and health and hospitals—are funded primarily through the state budget, while the main areas of priority decline—K-12 education and public safety—are funded through local budgets. Even highway spending seems to follow this pattern—split about 55-45 between state and local funding, its priority fell overall. But it was the *operating* component—where local government has a larger role—in which the relative priority fell; the capital component—in which state government plays a larger role—held its own. The expansion of spending on state programs may have been explicitly desired by the Commonwealth's voters, but it is also possible that it was at least in part an accident of the enormous growth in state revenues fueled by the economic expansion of the mid-1980s. The state's revenue base—largely based on sales, personal income, and corporate income—grew rapidly, permitting substantial growth in state-funded programs. By contrast, local revenues were held in check, tied to property taxes and limited by Proposition 2½.

What are Massachusetts' Value Choices Now?

Where did all of these changes leave Massachusetts by 1989? Massachusetts' pattern of spending is quite different than would be anticipated based on other states. Table 7-2 shows the difference between actual and benchmark spending for each spending area in

Table 7-2

Summary of Differences between Actual and Benchmark Spending Massachusetts, 1989[a]

	Numerical difference ($)[b]	Percent[c]	Rank (of 49)[d]
General Expenditures			
financed in state	+97 per capita	+3	11
Education			
Elementary and secondary	-200 per student	-4	21
Higher education	-1196 per student	-14	41
Human Services			
Direct assistance	+1017 per poor person	+56	3
Health and hospitals	+104 per capita	+75	2
Highways			
Operations	-24 per motor vehicle	-16	41
Total (including capital)	-137 per motor vehicle	-33	47
Public Safety and Corrections			
Public Safety	+9 per capita	+5	9
Corrections	-6 per capita	-7	27

[a] All dollar figures are adjusted for inflation and to remove state-to-state variations in input costs, and are expressed in real 1989 dollars.

[b] Actual minus benchmark spending, in units as shown.

[c] Actual minus benchmark spending as a percent of benchmark spending.

[d] Massachusetts' rank within the states ordered by the absolute difference of their actual spending from their individual benchmark spending.

1989, and shows Massachusetts' rank among the 49 states in relative priority shown toward each spending area measured as the difference between actual and benchmark spending. It seems fair to say that Massachusetts has a markedly different pattern of spending priorities than the average state.

Massachusetts' spending lies below its benchmark in both elementary and secondary education and in higher education. The priority toward K–12 education declined substantially during the 1980s, from $900 more than the benchmark per student to about $200 less than would be anticipated. The substantial *rise* in priority accorded to public higher education began from such a low base that it still left the Commonwealth spending nearly $1200 less per student than would be anticipated in a state with its circumstances and income, ranking behind 40 other states in terms of its relative effort.

Human services spending—where relative effort in Massachusetts increased during the 1980s—stood far above the benchmark in 1989. Direct assistance funded from in-state sources exceeded the benchmark by more than 50 percent; spending by the Commonwealth on health and hospitals programs, net of charges, exceeded what would be anticipated by 75 percent. Massachusetts ranks 3d and 2d, respectively, among the states in terms of the gap between its actual and benchmark spending in these areas. Massachusetts began the 1980s with a very high implicit valuation on human services, and increased that priority across the decade.

In highway spending, Massachusetts showed a low and falling relative priority. In overall spending, including capital projects, it spent about one-third less than would be anticipated, and ranked 47th out of the 49 sample states in relative priority. In highway operations, its relative priority fell from about average in 1979 to below 40 other states in 1989.

In public safety, Massachusetts spent about $10 per capita, about 5 percent, more than its benchmark. It began the period, however, with a very high degree of commitment, ranking 2d in the nation and spending about $50 per capita more than its (then much lower) benchmark. While its 1989 spending was more typical of what might be expected, its apparent valuation in this area has declined substantially.

Table 7-3 presents these results in terms of their aggregate impact on spending by state and local governments in Massachusetts in 1989. Figures presented in table 7-3 are in nominal terms, that is, the benchmark and actual figures presented in real terms elsewhere in this report have been re-adjusted to reflect Massachusetts' higher input costs. These figures are thus in what might be termed "budget" dollars, or budget expenditures required to achieve actual and benchmark service levels. In the aggregate, 1989 education spending in the Commonwealth was below the benchmark by about $350 million. Net human services spending exceeded the benchmark by about $1.4 billion. Total highways spending was below the benchmark by about $600 million. Public safety and corrections expenditures combined were about equal to the benchmark, with public safety expenditures about $60 million above the benchmark and corrections expenditures falling $40 million below.

According to the comparison between the spending conducted by Massachusetts and that of other states, Massachusetts values public spending on elementary and secondary education about as much as the average state, and higher education less than almost any other state. It values public spending on highways less than the great majority of other states. It values public spending on public safety about as much as do many other states, but considerably less than it did. And it values public spending on human services more—indeed, much more—than almost any other state.

If these are the values that the people of the Commonwealth want embodied in their public spending decisions, then they should be pleased. If these values came to be embodied in the Commonwealth's public spending by virtue of explicit consideration and deliberate choice, then we can be satisfied that the public spending allocation process is functioning well. If, instead, Massachusetts taxpayers do not find these values familiar, then changes need to be made. The

Table 7-3

Summary of Aggregate Budget Differences between Actual and Benchmark Spending, Massachusetts, 1989[a]

Spending Area	Nominal Spending Per Unit ($)		Number of Units	Total Expenditures (000 $)		Difference from Benchmark (000$)
	Actual	Benchmark		Actual	Benchmark	
General Expenditures financed in state	3,305 per capita	3,194 per capita	5,913,000 persons	19,545,000	18,888,005	+656,944
Education						
Elementary and secondary	5,105 per pupil	5,332 per pupil	814,000 pupils	4,155,730	4,339,933	- 184,203
Higher education	8,385 per pupil	9,739 per pupil	124,896 pupils	1,047,284	1,216,329	- 169,044
Human Services						
Direct assistance	3,210 per poor person	2,054 per poor person	629,802 poor persons	2,021,753	1,293,521	+728,231
Health and hospitals	275 per capita	157 per capita	5,913,000 persons	1,624,833	927,215	+697,619
Highways						
Operations	140 per vehicle	168 per vehicle	3,804,000 vehicles	531,761	637,181	- 105,421
Total (including capital)	291 per vehicle	448 per vehicle	3,804,000 vehicles	1,107,116	1,702,273	- 595,157
Public Safety and Corrections						
Public Safety	238 per capita	227 per capita	5,913,000 persons	1,405,638	1,343,755	+61,884
Corrections	88 per capita	94 per capita	5,913,000 persons	517,388	554,780	- 37,392

[a] Figures are *not* adjusted for state-to-state differences in input costs.

description offered in this study of the values currently embedded in Commonwealth spending is designed to serve as a point of departure, should change be needed.

Where from Here?

The comparisons made in this study—focusing on the gap between actual spending and benchmark spending based on the priorities exhibited by other states—provide a *description* of the choices, tastes, and values implicit in the level and pattern of public spending observed in Massachusetts. The description is *comparative*—that is, Massachusetts' values are described not absolutely, but only in relation to those exhibited by other states. The implicit values of other states are not a standard, they are merely a reference point, a way to describe Massachusetts' implicit spending choices.

This descriptive framework is *not* normative. The fact that Massachusetts' implicit public spending priorities are different from those of other states, as this study shows, does not imply that Massachusetts' choices are "wrong." There is no reason to expect that Massachusetts' priorities should be the same as those of other states; indeed, many live in Massachusetts precisely because it is different from other places. Some may also choose to be here because they like the value decisions implicit in public spending.

The description offered here is an attempt to provide a point of departure for a general deliberation on Massachusetts' overall spending priorities. *Value choices* should underlie the difficult budget decisions Massachusetts must make as it struggles to bring balance to its finances. People in Massachusetts differ widely from each other in the values they believe should inform those decisions. There is no prospect that all will agree. But as the debate is framed today, people also differ widely in their beliefs about the starting point—about what values are *currently* embodied in the spending now conducted. No study can tell people what values they should hold—that will remain a subject for individual reflection, public and private deliberation and argument. But a careful examination of current priorities can increase the general level of understanding as the point of departure for a conversation about what we want our values to be.

The policy recommendation that comes out of this study, then, is procedural. It suggests that leaders educate the public about the values currently embodied in Massachusetts' spending—values that are often obscured. Ultimately, the most important question is not where those values came from—it is whether they are the values taxpayers actually want. This study provides a description of Massachusetts' spending values, stated in terms of the differences between our values and those exhibited by other states. It is intended to be a comprehensible description of what the state is currently doing, stated in meaningful comparative terms. We can then ask, are these the values you want? Are these the values you thought were guiding public spending? If they are not, then in what direction would you propose that the state move from where it is now?

The purpose of this study is to *enable* such a discussion. It is up to the Commonwealth's political leadership to conduct it.

APPENDIX A

Methods and Approach

Many studies have compared the fiscal characteristics of Massachusetts to those of other states, both on the spending side and on the revenue side. Quite detailed comparisons of spending per capita in various expenditure areas and of tax revenues per capita or per $1000 of income for various taxes are available on an annual basis.[1] Many of these studies compare Massachusetts to an average of all states and to selected small groups of states (often referred to as "peer groups"). Behind the presentation of peer group comparisons lies the recognition that Massachusetts should not be expected to resemble the average of all of the other states.

While it does share many characteristics with at least some other states, Massachusetts is *atypical* in many quite important respects. Its citizens enjoy relatively high real incomes, and it has a relatively small population living in poverty; this can be expected to have an influence both on what level of public services the people of the state want and on the need to spend on programs designed to help those with low incomes. It has what is probably the best private secondary school system, and surely the best private higher education system, in the country; this might be expected to have an influence on the level of spending in the public schools. It has what is probably the greatest concentration of health care resources in the world; this might be expected to have an influence on the cost of health care provided

---

1 For two excellent examples, see the Massachusetts Taxpayers Foundation, *State Budget Trends,* Boston, various years, and the Governor's Management Task Force, *Massachusetts: Managing Our Future,* Boston, 1990. Each provides a broad and useful array of comparisons.

through public programs.[2] Its cost of living is above the national average; this may influence spending as well, particularly through the necessity to spend more per low-income family in order to provide a given standard of living. In part as a result of its high cost of living, and in reflection of its high real incomes, Massachusetts has relatively high average wages in the private sector; this could be expected to have an influence on the cost of producing public services, and therefore on the level of spending. Massachusetts has a relatively high proportion of elderly people; this can be expected to influence the level of spending on health, income support, housing, and nursing home programs. A comparison of Massachusetts to a broad average of other states, therefore, can be very difficult to interpret. With many important reasons to expect that spending in Massachusetts would differ from spending in other states, and with some of those reasons pointing in opposite directions, it is very difficult to know what to expect and what to be surprised by in such broad comparisons.

As a simple illustration, consider spending on elementary and secondary education through public schools. Figure A-1 shows a histogram of 49 states arrayed in terms of their state and local combined nominal K-12 public school spending per capita in 1989. As the figure indicates, about three-quarters of the states spent between $600 and $900 per capita; Massachusetts, with about $750 per capita, is approximately in the middle of the distribution, quite close to the national average. How should this be interpreted? The answer is that it is quite difficult to say. On the one hand, Massachusetts has a comparatively strong private elementary and secondary education sector, and it is possible that this might have some influence on the level of spending in the public sector. Perhaps more important, income in Massachusetts is comparatively high, and this should be

---

2 Having the greatest concentration of health care resources does not, of course, guarantee that it has the best health care for all of its citizens. Access to these resources is hardly uniform, and they are not necessarily organized in the best way possible to provide the best health status for the entire community.

Figure A-1

Nominal Elementary and Secondary Education Expenditures per Capita

1989

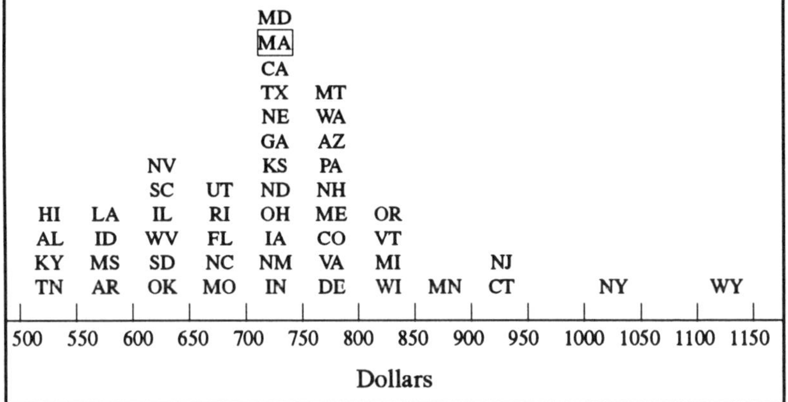

```
                        MD
                       |MA|
                        CA
                        TX   MT
                        NE   WA
                        GA   AZ
             NV         KS   PA
             SC   UT    ND   NH
   HI   LA   IL   RI    OH   ME   OR
   AL   ID   WV   FL    IA   CO   VT
   KY   MS   SD   NC    NM   VA   MI        NJ
   TN   AR   OK   MO    IN   DE   WI   MN   CT        NY        WY
   |    |    |    |    |    |    |    |    |    |    |    |    |    |
  500  550  600  650  700  750  800  850  900  950 1000 1050 1100 1150
                              Dollars
```

expected to increase spending on education (as well as on other public services). In addition, Massachusetts faces substantially higher than average wage costs. How, when they are all combined, should these influences affect public spending? Once these differences have been allowed for, is Massachusetts' spending higher or lower than expected? It is very hard to say, based on a simple per capita comparison with other states.

Moreover, as a result of the many important ways in which it is not typical, Massachusetts has few true peers among states. A seemingly natural (and frequently used) comparison group is the New England states, but even a cursory glance around New England reveals profound economic, social, and political culture differences. Indeed, one might be hard pressed to identify a geographically natural region with *more* diversity—ranging from politically conservative, high-per-capita-income New Hampshire, through low-income but moderately liberal Maine, to high-income and quite liberal Connecticut and Massachusetts, with Rhode Island and Vermont each different in their own special ways from all of the others. Even the comparison of Massachusetts to Connecticut, in many ways the most natural pairing of New England states, is difficult. Connecticut has high average incomes in part because of a concentration of high-income people along the border with New York; this phenomenon appears to be related to the form and level of personal income taxation in New York City and New York State, and therefore probably exerts a material influence on the tax and public spending preferences of the state. It has no real analogue in the Massachusetts context (if anything, Massachusetts is on the opposite side of this phenomenon, with some wealthy people from the state choosing for tax reasons to locate in New Hampshire and Florida).

Other comparisons of Massachusetts to selected groups of states are similarly fraught with ambiguity. For example, because of the strong "high-tech" orientation of some of Massachusetts' economy, it is often compared to other states whose economies have significant technology components. While this may be useful for some limited comparisons, as a general yardstick it again raises substantial difficulties in interpretation. Commonly identified high-tech states include California, Texas, and North Carolina; while each has a significant technology-based economy, each also has a substantial agricultural economy, which presumably shapes both public service needs and community preferences, and has no analogue in the Massachusetts setting.[3] For example, it may be much more sensible to compare the

---

3 Indeed, if one considers the list "California, Maryland, Massachusetts, North Carolina, Texas, and Washington" and asks, what do these states have in common?, partial reliance on high-tech industries is one of only a small number of plausible answers that could be given; these states share few other major characteristics. Thus, this is perhaps best used as a peer group with regard to characteristics of public spending and taxation that can be expected to be closely related to technology industries. Texas and North Carolina have quite low costs of living, while parts of California and Massachusetts have among the highest costs of living in the nation. Other salient differences abound. It is not clear what implications should be drawn from findings that Massachusetts differs in some material way from the average of such a disparate collection of other states.

level of funding per student within the higher education system that goes into high-technology curricula than to compare the level of per recipient spending on cash assistance programs across these states.

A New Approach

Comparing Massachusetts to other states meaningfully is not as easy as computing simple averages; we need a more carefully chosen yardstick than the average spending of a selected group of other states. No matter how the comparison group of states is selected, there will remain important differences between the circumstances faced by Massachusetts and the states in the peer group, and the comparison will therefore be difficult to interpret.

In comparisons formed in the traditional way, spending in Massachusetts is compared to what other states spend, given *their* circumstances. It is more difficult, but potentially much more useful, to compare the spending Massachusetts actually does to the spending that Massachusetts would be expected to do, given *its own* circumstances. Thus, instead of using the other states and their circumstances as a comparative benchmark, the *pattern* of spending in other states would be used as a means of determining how we should expect spending to vary as a result of important systematic influences (circumstances like the number of poor people, the number of students enrolled in public schools, and so on). The pattern observed among the other states would then be applied to Massachusetts, to compute the level of spending that would be expected *given Massachusetts' own circumstances,* if spending here followed the same pattern as it does in other states. Since the pattern observed in other states embodies the level and mix of priorities that they collectively give to spending in each area, this comparative benchmark indicates the spending that would be expected if Massachusetts exhibited spending priorities similar to those in the other states, but adjusting for the fact that Massachusetts faces its own specific circumstances that are in many important and systematic ways different from those of other states.

This study provides this new kind of comparison. Data on public spending in other states are used indirectly to provide a comparative benchmark. The pattern of public spending observed across other states is used to construct two crucial inputs for the analysis: 1) a set of "baseline" or average priorities about the level and mix of spending across different public services, and 2) estimates of how spending varies as a function of important socioeconomic determinants of public spending.[4] Starting with the indicated average priorities shown by the other states, and adjusting for Massachusetts' differing circumstances as indicated by the observed pattern of how those circumstances affect spending in other states, this study constructs a comparative benchmark based on Massachusetts' own characteristics. It thus focuses attention on the difference between Massachusetts' actual spending and benchmark spending for Massachusetts based on

---

4   This approach is related to a method used extensively in the public finance literature, generally referred to as an "expenditure study," though it is used here for a somewhat different purpose. Traditional expenditure studies typically seek to explain as high a fraction of the variation in spending from jurisdiction to jurisdiction as possible, and use a combination of political culture and fiscal need variables. They are generally concerned with being able to describe what expenditure variations are correlated with—and in predicting what expenditures will be. By contrast, this study is concerned with separating the influence of fiscal need variables from political culture variables, and thus isolating the influence of priority choices. For an interesting example of the traditional form of public expenditure study, and a good survey of other early work on techniques of this form, see Roy W. Bahl, *Metropolitan City Expenditures: A Comparative Analysis* (Lexington, KY: University of Kentucky Press, 1969). For an example more closely related to the work presented here, see Katharine L. Bradbury, Helen F. Ladd, Mark Perrault, Andrew Reschovsky, and John Yinger, "State Aid to Offset Fiscal Disparities Across Communities," *National Tax Journal*, Vol. 37, No. 2, 151–170. For an alternative way to adjust for differing fiscal circumstances across states, see Robert W. Rafuse, Jr., *Representative Expenditures: Addressing the Neglected Dimension of Fiscal Capacity*, Advisory Commission on Intergovernmental Relations, Washington, DC, December 1990.

spending observed in other states, making allowances for relevant differences.

This comparison, if it is carefully developed, can be interpreted as an indication of the difference between the priorities exhibited in Massachusetts and the priorities exhibited on average by other states. Simple comparisons of Massachusetts' spending to average spending by other states *cannot* be interpreted as an indication of relative priority, because they do not allow for any of the quite important and systematic differences that drive public spending. Once allowances for those factors are introduced, the comparison can be quite different from what the simple contrast of averages might seem to suggest. *This study is not based on a direct comparison of Massachusetts to any other state or average of other states.* Instead, it is based on a comparison of Massachusetts to *itself,* to the spending that would be expected to take place, after making adjustments for the circumstances we actually face, if Massachusetts had the average spending priorities exhibited by other states.

Constructing the Right Comparison

To construct this more illuminating comparison, we need to separate the observed difference between spending in Massachusetts and spending in other states into three components: 1) differences that are due to *costs,* 2) differences that are due to *circumstances,* and 3) differences that are due to *choices.*

The first category includes any differences in spending levels that are due to regional differences in costs. To the extent that some states must pay more for the inputs required to provide public services, higher spending is not a reflection of a higher priority placed upon that public service, but merely of the extra effort required to meet the challenges of higher costs. To ensure that we are examining real differences in the level of priority, we must adjust the expenditure data for input cost differences.

Once the data are adjusted for input cost differences, there are two further reasons spending levels will differ across states. Some states face more challenging problems than others. These states—with higher populations of poor people or medically needy elderly people—should be expected to make greater public service expenditures than states with small numbers of poor people and younger, rapidly expanding work-age populations. These factors—collectively referred to in this study as "circumstances" of the state's public service landscape—must also be allowed for in order to determine the relative emphasis the state puts on spending in each area as a matter of choice. If we find a state has higher expenditures on nursing care because it has a higher proportion of elderly people in its population, we cannot properly say that it shows a great emphasis on health programs unless it still seems to have high spending *after* adjusting for the greater fiscal needs it faces.

Once the influence of cost differences and differences due to circumstances are removed, the remaining difference can be ascribed to "choices." The choices component can be identified as the difference between the (cost-adjusted) actual spending in Massachusetts and the level of (cost-adjusted) spending that would be expected on the basis of the priorities shown by other states, adjusting for the circumstances that Massachusetts actually faces. Technically, the divergence between the actual spending observed in Massachusetts and the estimated benchmark level constructed for Massachusetts on the basis of the other states can be interpreted as an indication that a) there are important systematic differences between Massachusetts and other states that were not measured and, if included in the study, would indicate further necessary allowances for differences in circumstances, and/or b) Massachusetts' spending embodies a relative priority different from that exhibited by other states. In order to make sure that the component identified as largely due to *choices* is accurately described, we must be careful to construct the adjustments for the portion identified as *circumstances* accurately.

Adjusting for Differences in Costs[5]

The costs of inputs used to produce public services vary substantially across states, and therefore are a circumstance faced by states that can be expected to have an influence on public spending. (An immediate problem with most traditional comparisons of expenditures across states is that they ignore these differences in cost levels, and therefore present comparisons that mix real differences in public service levels together with differences that reflect only that one state has to spend more to purchase the same services.) For example, the local cost of living is substantially higher in Massachusetts than in Texas; to maintain the same standard of living for a recipient of public welfare, Massachusetts would have to spend more. Similarly, if wages are higher than, say, in Iowa, then Massachusetts should be expected to spend more on education to be able to provide the same real level of services.

Correcting for these cost differences is an important element of forming correct comparisons between states. *The public expenditure data used in this study were adjusted for cost differences on the basis of input costs before any analysis was conducted.* That is, facing its particular relative costs of inputs was implicitly regarded as an unavoidable circumstance for each state. If a particular state had to pay 10 percent more to purchase the inputs to make a given level of service in a particular expenditure area, then its expenditures were deflated by 10 percent to reflect the actual service level purchasable

---

5   The methods and data used to construct the cost adjustments described in this section are described in greater technical detail in appendix B. Robert Rafuse, in a study conducted for the ACIR and designed to compare expenditures across states, developed the method of cost adjustments adapted with some modifications for use in this study. See Robert W. Rafuse, *Representative Expenditures: Addressing the Neglected Dimension of Fiscal Capacity,* Advisory Commission on Intergovernmental Relations, Washington, DC, 1990.

through its expenditures rather than the nominal amount of its spending.

Input costs were identified in three categories: 1) wages, 2) the general cost of living, and 3) health care services. The component of each public service expenditure that was composed of wage payments to public sector workers was deflated by the relative wages of *private* workers in each state.[6] The component of public spending in each area going for general purchases of services from the private sector or for cash payments was adjusted by a local cost-of-living index. The component going to pay for health services was adjusted by a local health care cost index based on the health sector's proportion of wages and other costs.

The input-cost-adjusted expenditure data on which the analysis in this study was conducted can be thought of as embodying the "public services purchasing power expended" by each jurisdiction. By adjusting for input costs, we in effect anticipate that states with higher costs will spend more but will not be influenced by those higher costs to purchase lower real levels of service than they otherwise would. If states respond to higher implicit prices by conserving on public services, then their cost-adjusted expenditures do not reflect their actual priorities, but instead their priorities adjusted by the influence of costs. This implies that the relative priority on public spending is probably understated for states facing high costs and overstated for states with low costs. In general, given the range of input costs observed, this effect can be expected to be relatively small.

---

6 Wages for private sector workers were used because they represent the cost of services in the labor pool out of which public workers must be drawn. If a state chooses to pay its public workers differently than would be indicated by the prevailing private sector wages, that difference should be thought of as a public spending choice, and it should not be adjusted for. Instead, it should appear as part of the remaining difference when other factors have been allowed for.

Efficiency

It should be noted that no adjustment has been made for the relative efficiency with which states turn public services purchasing effort into actual public services. Some states may be less efficient in turning a (cost-adjusted) dollar of spending into a dollar of service value. Ideally, expenditures in each state should be adjusted for the relative efficiency with which they are spent; this would result in a measure of public services actually purchased. Unfortunately, no consistent and reliable data on relative governmental efficiency or performance across states and across time exist for *any* spending area. Thus, we are forced to assume that efficiency is constant both across states and across time. This means that the study presented here concentrates on public services purchasing power expended, not on public service levels actually provided. The result of this focus is probably to understate the actual priority for public spending in communities with relatively low efficiency; given their lower efficiency, they may well expend less effort on public services than they would like to, because they get less service per unit of purchasing effort expended.

Separating Fiscal Circumstances from Choices

A wide variety of factors can be expected to influence the level of public spending, ranging from direct needs to indicators of the general political culture or propensity to use government programs to address social problems. For example, the number of families with incomes below the poverty level is clearly an indicator of a fiscal circumstance that is addressed to some degree through public spending in every state. Of course, different states make widely differing choices about how completely to meet the needs of such families through public programs. Thus, indicators of the state's political culture—for example, the voting record of the state's congressional delegation and the proportion of Democrats and Republicans in the state legislature—are likely to explain an important component of the variation in spending observed across states. The influence of political culture, of course, reflects the value choices of the state. Thus, in forming the benchmark it is important to allow for the effects of the fiscal circumstances while holding aside the impacts of political culture.

To separate these influences, they must first be jointly estimated.[7] This is accomplished by identifying, for each area of expenditure, two sets of explanatory variables: 1) a set of fiscal indicators relevant to that area of spending, and 2) a collection of political culture indicators. (Since the political culture is not specific to different spending areas, the same collection of political culture variables is used for all spending areas.) The pattern of spending as a function of both fiscal circumstance and political culture variables is then estimated by linear regression using data from the 49 sample states for the eleven-year period from 1979 through 1989. The linear regression statistical procedure is designed to separate a variety of different influences and attribute the independent effect of each influence to its corresponding explanatory variable.

Once the size of these independent influences has been estimated, the benchmark can be formed. The benchmark for any particular state is created by taking the national average for spending in the area in question and adjusting it by the estimated impact of each fiscal need variable times the difference between the state's actual value of that fiscal need variable and the national average value for that variable. For example, suppose the national average for spending in a given area is $500 per capita and that the estimated impact on spending in that area from having a higher than average level of poor families is $100 of spending per capita for each additional one percentage point difference in the fraction of families who are living below the poverty

---

7 The effects of political culture and circumstances must be jointly estimated because they may be (and probably are) correlated with each other. Omitting the political culture variables would result in attributing their effects to the circumstances variables with which they are correlated, thus (probably) overstating the adjustments that should be made as a result of differing circumstances. I am grateful to Katharine Bradbury for suggesting this approach.

line. Then a state with 2 percent more families living in poverty than the national average would have benchmark spending $200 per capita higher than the national average, or $700 per capita. The benchmark is *not* adjusted to reflect differences between the state and the national average in political culture. In effect, the benchmark is formed as if the state had the average political culture observed across the 49 sample states. It is in this sense that the benchmark represents the spending that would be expected if the state made its choices according to the values of the average state, but faced its own particular fiscal need circumstances.

To state this approach more precisely, let

y_{it} be the input-cost-adjusted spending by state i in period t in the spending area being examined;

X_{it} be a collection of circumstances variables;

P_{it} be a collection of political culture variables; and

T_t be a linear trend variable $(1, 2, \ldots 11)$.

The coefficients are estimated by ordinary least squares regression from the relationship

$$y = \alpha + X\beta + P\gamma + T\varphi + T^2\psi + \varepsilon \tag{1}$$

The benchmark estimate for spending by state i in period t is then

$$y_{it}^b = \hat{\alpha} + X_{it}\hat{\beta} + \overline{P_t}\hat{\gamma} + T_t\hat{\varphi} + T_t^2\hat{\psi} \tag{2}$$

where

y_{it}^b is the benchmark estimate;

X_{it} is the actual circumstances values for state i in period t;

$\overline{P_t}$ is the average political culture value for all states in period t;

T_t is the trend value for period t; and

$\hat{\alpha}$, $\hat{\beta}$, $\hat{\gamma}$, $\hat{\varphi}$ and $\hat{\psi}$ are the estimated coefficients from equation (1).

The benchmark value can also be written in deviations form as

$$y_{it}^{b} = (X_{it}-\overline{X}_{t})\hat{\beta}+\hat{\alpha}+\overline{X}_{t}\,\hat{\beta}+\overline{P}_{t}\hat{\gamma}+T_{t}\hat{\varphi}+T_{t}^{2}\hat{\psi} \qquad (3)$$

$$= (X_{it}-\overline{X}_{t})\hat{\beta}+\hat{y}_{t} \qquad (4)$$

where $\overline{X}_{t}$ is the average circumstances value for all states in period t; and

$$\hat{y}_{t} = \hat{\alpha}+\overline{X}_{t}\,\hat{\beta}+\overline{P}_{t}\hat{\gamma}+T_{t}\hat{\varphi}+T_{t}^{2}\hat{\psi}$$

is the estimated spending by a state with average circumstances and political culture in period *t*.

Equation 4 thus says that the benchmark for state *i* in period *t* is the estimated national average for period *t*, adjusted by the estimated spending pattern (embodied in the estimated circumstances coefficient $\hat{\beta}$) times the difference between state *i*'s actual circumstances and the national average circumstances in that period.

Selection of Explanatory Variables

In order to be able to interpret the difference between actual and benchmark spending as an indication of the relative priority or choice embodied in the state's spending in that area of public services, rather than as a reflection of the influence of unmeasured circumstances that should have been allowed for, we must be confident that 1) the measured influences can be expected to capture the major structural reasons why spending in Massachusetts differs, and 2) the political culture variables adequately capture the choice differences across states. Thus, considerable care has been taken in the selection of political culture variables and in choosing the structural fiscal need influences to be factored out.

Structural needs for spending must be allowed for. For example, in forming the benchmark for public assistance programs (a significant component of which is in support of nursing home care for the elderly), we must be sure to account for the influence of having a larger or smaller number of elderly people in the state's population.

We must also include variables to capture the influence of political culture, in order to make sure that the effects of differences in spending that are due to political culture differences are not erroneously attributed to differences in fiscal circumstance variables. For example, the southern states are often observed to have a different set of attitudes about taxes and public services than states in New England. Southern states also have a higher fraction of families living in poverty. Leaving out the political culture variables, or a variable indicating which region a state is located in, would thus be likely to cause a portion of the impact of what is actually a political culture difference to be attributed as an effect of having a higher fraction of families living in poverty. It is, therefore, important to include both fiscal need and political culture variables when estimating the spending pattern across the states, even though in forming the benchmark each state will be treated as if it had the average value of each of the political culture variables. This implies that care must be taken not only in the process of identifying which variables to include in the statistical estimation process, but also in deciding which to treat as fiscal circumstances and which to treat as indicators of political culture.

This issue is especially difficult to resolve when some of the regional differences can be expected to arise as a result of variations in the real cost of providing public services. Spending on transportation provides a good example. We might expect that the real cost of providing roads is lower in the South than in northern states as a result of climate. Climatic conditions and the effects of the weather on road systems are not choices made by states; they are non-choice circumstances states must face (indeed, overcome), in order to provide a given level of real service to their citizens. If, however, we adjust for this difference in real costs by including a regional indicator variable, that variable may capture both taste differences and real service cost differences, which we are trying to separate. To address this difficulty, we include a geographic location indicator to capture the political culture effects that vary by regions, and also include a measure'designed to capture more specifically the climatic influence for which we are trying to allow. (In the case of transportation spending, this means including a variable measuring the severity of winter weather, called "heating degree days," commonly used by utility companies to estimate energy utilization in winter.) By including both, we permit the statistical estimation process to separate the political culture impacts from the climatic impacts. (Even though these effects are correlated, the linear regression process is designed to estimate and attribute the separate independent components of the effects as accurately as possible.) We then treat the climate variable as a fiscal need component, allowing differences in this variable to move each state's benchmark, but treat the region indicator as a political culture variable, setting its value equal to the national average in forming the benchmark for each state.[8] There is no perfect way to maintain this separation, however; as the example of transportation spending indicates, the relevant measure of circumstance differences (heating degree days) will be quite strongly related to location (southern states have low values for heating degree days; northern states have high values), and thus even the best statistical process for separating these influences may not be able to distinguish them with complete accuracy.

The problem, then, is to determine *which* influences to include in examining the pattern of spending in each area of public services—

---

8 Technically, this is carried out by including a full set of regional dummy
   variables in the political culture variables P in equation (1); these dummy
   variables capture both the constant term α and the regional variations
   unaccounted for by other political culture variables or by the circumstances
   variables.

that is, to determine which variables to include and to decide whether a given variable is more likely to be capturing differences in the need for public services, or in the real cost of providing public services, or is instead capturing aspects of local preference or priority for spending. Many variables that might explain more of the variation in spending would be doing so precisely because they were measuring differences in the priority given by states to various areas of public spending.[9]

Income as an Explanatory Variable

A related issue of interpretation is raised by the inclusion of income as one of the circumstances whose impact is allowed for in establishing the Massachusetts benchmark spending in each area. Income is commonly found to be an important determinant of the level of public and private spending. Massachusetts differs markedly from most other states in the level of its income, and therefore allowing for this difference will often have a sizable impact on the location of the benchmark. But having more income does not generate a fiscal need; if anything, as privately available resources increase we might expect to see the need for public spending decline. Whether or not to spend the additional income that Massachusetts' citizens have on public

---

9 The use of the percentage of elderly people in the population provides a good example of a variable that may capture both needs and tastes. Many public programs are designed to meet the needs of the elderly, and having a larger elderly population can therefore be expected to generate greater needs for public spending. But the presence of a larger proportion of elderly voters may also produce a shift in level and mix of public spending priorities. To the extent that a variable designed to adjust for differences in fiscal need levels *also* captures some part of differences in public spending preferences, the interpretation of the difference between benchmark and actual spending shifts. For example, suppose that the number of elderly people in a state can be expected to influence its political culture. Then instead of measuring all spending priority choices, the gap between benchmark and actual spending would measure differences between Massachusetts' choices and those of other states *beyond* those choice differences that would be anticipated to result from having a larger elderly population.

services could quite naturally be interpreted as one of their public services choices.

Whether or not to include income as a structural explanatory variable depends entirely upon the intended interpretation of the remaining difference between the benchmark and the actual spending observed in the state. Observing the pattern of public services spending across other states indicates that higher income states generally spend more on public services. If the benchmark is formed without reference to income, a consistent and large component of the gap in most areas of spending will be attributable to the fact that Massachusetts is a high-income state, and generally chooses to behave that way. It seems more natural to construct the benchmark for Massachusetts with a recognition that it is a high-income state, and to view its actual spending against that backdrop, rather than to construct the benchmark as if Massachusetts were an average-income state, and constantly observe that there is a large gap, a high fraction of which is accounted for by income. Because adjustment for income is a different kind of adjustment than the other structural allowances made on the basis of fiscal need and cost factors, however, the influence of income as a determinant of the benchmark is separately noted, and readers who wish to reinterpret the spending of income as a choice can reconstruct the estimated difference between benchmark and actual spending accordingly.

Over the course of the period examined in this study, real per capita income changed markedly in Massachusetts, rising by about 40 percent, a larger increase than experienced by any other state but one over the same period. Income is indeed an important determinant of public spending patterns, but it is not obvious that a state with rapidly rising income should necessarily adjust its public service spending package to immediately accommodate its changing income circumstances, in the way that would be indicated by observing the relationship between income and spending across states. That is, if comparing spending across states shows that a 10 percent increase in income leads to a 5 percent increase in spending in a particular expenditure area, we need not conclude that a state whose income rises by 10 percent will immediately increase its public service purchases in that area by 5 percent; the adjustment may take place over a number of years. To allow for this possibility, two concepts of income were used in forming benchmark spending for Massachusetts. The first, per capita income, uses the actual real income for each year. The second, permanent income, uses the average income across the entire sample period in every year—that is, it presumes that the public service package is a reflection of the community's average income over time, not of its actual income in a particular year. These two assumptions frame the extremes of hypotheses about how the state might be expected to adjust its public service packages to changes in its income situation, and might therefore be regarded as indicating the range of possible benchmarks that could be produced by entertaining hypotheses that mix permanent and transitory components of income. In practice, the difference between the benchmark estimates for these two concepts was nearly always quite small. As a result, in the results detailed in this report, the per capita income concept will be the focus of the analysis.

There is no obvious reason to expect that the effect of income on spending will be linear. In explanatory analyses, the income effect was specified more generally, allowing for a curved rather than linear relationship. The results did not appear to be materially different, so in the analyses presented here a linear income effect was included.

The General National Time Trend

In nearly every area of public spending, there is a general trend observed across the country for real spending to increase across the decade. Since income is also rising steadily in most states, the general trend is likely to be attributed to rising income, thus overstating the effect of income in the analysis, if a general trend is not allowed for. In each expenditure pattern estimation, therefore, a general time trend was included. Since there is no strong reason to presume that the general trend is linear—that is, adds (or subtracts) the same increment to spending between each two years—a nonlinear (quadratic) time trend was estimated. For some spending areas, estimates were also produced using more general functional forms for the time trend. Generally, there was only a small difference between the benchmark estimates produced with linear, quadratic, or more sophisticated time trends.

Selecting Fiscal Need Variables

The approach taken in this study to constructing the benchmark spending for Massachusetts is to allow for a relatively small number of relevant structural influences in each spending area. Moreover, most of the explanatory variables used are drawn from a short list of state characteristics that can be expected to have an influence on several areas of spending. Table A-1 shows the variables most commonly used in this study. For example, the real cost of providing a broad array of public services may be different in metropolitan and rural areas; as a result, this influence is observed and adjusted for in a variety of spending areas. In each area of spending, the measured influences will include those from the general list of fiscal need indicators that appear relevant to that area, augmented where necessary by indicators specific to that area of spending. Generally, only a small number of influences will be allowed for.

Table A-1

Commonly Used Explanatory Variables

Fiscal Needs Indicator Variables
    Poverty population
    Elderly population
    School-age population
    Students enrolled in schools
    Fraction of population living in metropolitan areas

Other Circumstance Variables
    Per capita income
    Time trend

This parsimonious approach to allowing for systematic differences runs some risk of overlooking important areas of difference in circumstances that should be thought of as outside the realm of choice or "determining priorities" in public spending. It minimizes the risk, however, that the collection of variables treated as fiscal circumstance indicators will be capturing not only differences in structural needs and circumstantial reasons for variations in public spending, but also variations in value choices.

Selecting Political Culture Indicators

The purpose of the political culture variables is to permit estimation of the influence of political value choices made by each state on the level of public spending. Thus, indicators more or less directly related to the public finance propensities of the state are to be preferred over more general sociological indicators. Political scientists have created and used a variety of such measures in studies of public spending, and this study relies on measures that are common in that literature.[10] The measures include what is perhaps the most extensively used single index of political culture, the Elazar index (developed in the late 1960s by Ira Sharkansky based on the earlier work of Daniel Elazar).[11] The average value of the Americans for Democratic Action's "liberal quotient"—a score computed and published each year for each member of Congress, designed to indicate how often he or she voted in keeping with the ADA's preferred position on legislation—for the members of each state's congressional delegation is also included. In addition, the fraction of Democrats in the state legislature, the party affiliation of the governor, the gender composition of the legislature, and an index of the powers of the governor with respect to spending are included. An indicator of which

---

10 Appendix B contains a more detailed discussion of the sources and definitions of the political culture variables used in this study.

11 Because there is no reason to expect that the Elazar index will have a linear impact on spending, this variable was entered in a nonlinear (quadratic) form.

geographic region the state belongs to is also included to capture any regional political predispositions toward public spending. Table A-2 provides a list of the collection of political culture variables used in each spending pattern estimation.

Table A-2

Political Culture Variables

Elazar political culture index
Average of state's congressional delegation's ADA rating
Fraction of Democrats in state legislature
Fraction of women in state legislature
Party affiliation of state governor
Index of fiscal powers of the governor
Region of the country to which the state belongs

Characterizing the Gap

In general, the allowances made for differences in structural circumstances will involve a relatively small set of influences. This raises the possibility that not all important systematic non-taste differences will have been measured. Technically, the difference between the actual spending in Massachusetts and the computed benchmark spending level includes any remaining unmeasured circumstantial differences *and* the difference between the tastes exhibited by Massachusetts in its spending and those exhibited by other states. We might call this "differences due to unmeasured circumstances and choices." To the extent that the major structural influences and differences in circumstances that determine public service needs have been accurately measured, the gap principally measures Massachusetts' public spending *choices*. It compares the priorities Massachusetts gives to various areas of public service to the priorities shown by the other states. Rather than repeat the technical description of the gap as "the remaining difference unexplained by the chosen non-taste structural and circumstances variables," the gap will be referred to as an indication of public services spending priority not accounted for by measured fiscal needs or circumstances. The language of "choices" should be understood throughout this study in this technical sense. Any reader who believes that a major structural influence was omitted should adjust his or her interpretation of the gap—and the language used to describe the gap—accordingly.

Sensitivity of the Estimates

Since the benchmark spending for each public service is established on the basis of an observed pattern of spending across other states, it is clearly a function of precisely what pattern is examined. Different choices of explanatory variables would yield somewhat different estimates of the benchmark for any given year, and thus to somewhat different estimates of the gap between actual and benchmark spending, referred to here as an indication of the relative priority shown by the state toward spending in that area. Substituting a different measure of a given explanatory variable (for example, using average family income rather than per capita income) generally has a very small impact on the estimated benchmark, but more substantial changes in the explanatory variables or in the independent variables (for example, changing the input cost or local cost of living adjustments, changing the form of the dependent variable, or deciding to include an additional explanatory variable like the number of miles of mass transit service in the highways equation) can often raise or lower the benchmark by as much as 5 percent or more. In general, however, the pattern of actual spending in comparison to the benchmark is less subject to change than the level of the benchmark. Thus, we may be better able to observe *changes* in spending priorities in Massachusetts than we are to describe precisely what the *level* of the priority is in comparison to other states.[12] Moreover, even though the

---

12 This reinforces the general point that the analysis performed here is *descriptive* rather than *normative*. The level of priority shown by other states

adjustments and corrections presented and used here are both estimated and imperfect, they will almost certainly provide a much better basis for comparison of spending among states than unadjusted per capita or per dollar of income figures that make no allowance for the systematically differing circumstances of each state.

Form of the Estimating Equations

Various forms of the estimating equations were used, depending upon the area of spending under consideration. The scale of the state—the size of its population or other relevant need group—is obviously an important determinant of the level of spending. Thus, the dependent variable in each area was stated either in per capita terms or in terms of spending per person in the relevant needs group. For example, the dependent variable in the equations estimating elementary and secondary school expenditures was stated in terms of the (cost-adjusted, real) spending per student enrolled in public schools. By contrast, the dependent variable in the equations estimating expenditures in public welfare (an area of human services that includes cash assistance programs as well as Medicaid expenditures) was stated in terms of the spending per person living below the poverty level.

The independent variables in the estimating equations were correspondingly stated in terms either of per capita or per member of the relevant needs group where that was appropriate. For example, in an equation estimating the per capita general operating expenditures of state and local government as a function of the number of elderly people in the state, the independent variable indicating the needs as

is in no obvious sense the *right* level of priority for Massachusetts to show—Massachusetts must decide on its own what level of priority is right for it. Having a description of how the priority appears to have been shifting over time, however, may be very useful—in particular, it can frame the question of whether value choices are being made systematically, consciously, and accountably, on the one hand, or more or less randomly, on the other.

a function of the number of elderly people was stated in terms of the percentage of the population that was elderly. Similarly, in an equation estimating public expenditures on public welfare as a function of the number of female-headed households in the state, where the dependent variable was stated in terms of spending per poor person, the density of female-headed households was also stated in terms of the number of such households relative to the size of the population living below the poverty line.

Reporting the Results

The most straightforward way to use the estimated benchmark for a particular state is to compare it to actual spending; this gives a direct measure of the priority shown toward a given spending area. But the benchmarks and estimated spending patterns can also be used to examine the relative priority shown towards a spending area by one state in comparison to others, to see why a state differs from the national average, and to see how it has changed over time. Four approaches are used repeatedly in this study. These approaches will be described in detail here, using figures and tables from chapter 2.

Figure 2-2 gives an example of the first approach, showing a plot of Massachusetts' actual spending and its estimated benchmark for elementary and secondary education operating expenditures per pupil over the period 1979 to 1989. All figures are in real terms, adjusted for input costs, and reported in 1989 real dollars. (This means that "actual" spending in each year is *not* the nominal amount Massachusetts spent in that year. Instead it is the amount Massachusetts spent, adjusted for input costs and reported in 1989 dollars for every year.) The gap between benchmark and actual spending provides an indication of how much Massachusetts was expending, in real education services purchasing power, in comparison to what would be expected if it shared other states' average value choices in K–12 education.

Since the gap between its actual and benchmark spending in any given year can be interpreted as a measure of each state's priority, the relative priority can be examined by comparing these gaps across

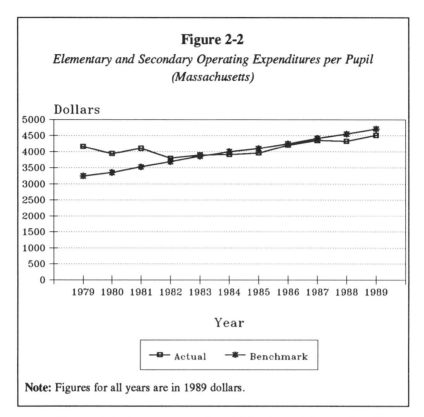

Figure 2-2

Elementary and Secondary Operating Expenditures per Pupil (Massachusetts)

Note: Figures for all years are in 1989 dollars.

states. Figure 2-1 gives an example of this view of the results. Here, each state is plotted according to the size of the gap between actual and benchmark spending in 1979 and in 1989. Thus, for example, Rhode Island and New Jersey are shown in 1979 as spending between $600 and $700 per K–12 student *more* than their respective benchmarks (in real, input-cost-adjusted terms); Alabama and Missouri are shown as spending between $500 and $600 *less* than their respective benchmarks in 1979. The distribution of states in terms of their spending relative to their benchmarks provides an indication of how wide the dispersion in priority shown toward elementary and secondary education is across states.

The spending pattern estimates also permit an examination of the components that explain why a given state's spending differs from

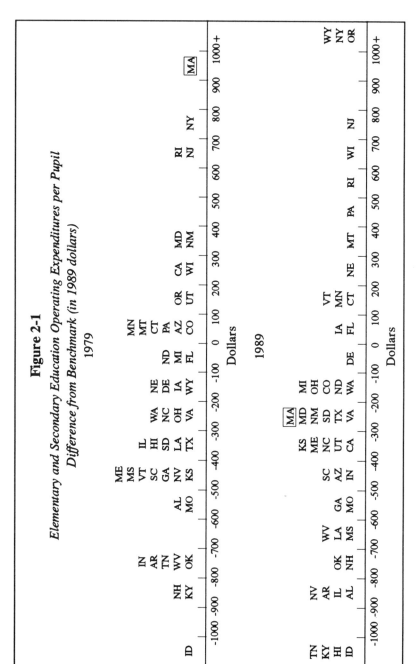

Figure 2-1

Elementary and Secondary Education Operating Expenditures per Pupil
Difference from Benchmark (in 1989 dollars)

the national average. Table 2-1 shows an example of such a decomposition. The table begins with the estimated national average spending for 1989 (this corresponds to $\hat{y}_t$ in equation (4)). In 1989, Massachusetts' input costs were 13 percent higher for K–12 education, so to reach the national average of $4554, Massachusetts would have to spend $597 more in nominal dollars. Next, the table reports the impact of differences in circumstances, divided into fiscal needs circumstances and per capita income circumstances (together, these correspond to $(X_{it} - \overline{X}_t)\hat{\beta}$ in equation (4)). In total, these differences suggest that Massachusetts would spend $110 + $51 = $161 more

Table 2-1

Reconciliation of National Average to Massachusetts Spending
Public Elementary and Secondary Education Operating Spending per
Enrolled Student, 1989

	Spending per enrolled student (1989 dollars)	Percent of national average
National average spending		
Nominal national average	4554	100
Adjustment to national average		
for Massachusetts input costs	597	13
Differences in circumstances		
Fiscal need indicators	110	2
Per capita income	51	1
Input costs associated with		
differences due to circumstances	21	0
Differences in choices		
Choice differences	-200	-4
Input costs associated with		
differences due to choices	-26	-1
Nominal Massachusetts 1989		
spending	5105	112

in real terms than the national average; because it faces higher input costs, this would also require spending an additional $21 per student in nominal dollars. Finally, the table shows the remaining differences, the gap between benchmark and actual spending of $200 in real terms. The fact that Massachusetts chooses to spend $200 less per student in real terms than its benchmark also saves it an additional 26 nominal dollars because of its higher input costs. In combination, these components reconcile the difference between the national average and Massachusetts' actual nominal spending in 1989.

This table also provides a way to remove the effect of income from the construction of the 1989 benchmark. As the table indicates, the 1989 benchmark for K–12 education was raised $51 by allowing for the effect of income; without this effect, the benchmark would have been closer to actual spending. Massachusetts' actual spending fell below its income-*un*adjusted benchmark by $200 - $51 = $149 in 1989.[13]

We can also use the estimated spending patterns to identify the components of change in a state's spending over time. Table 2-2 provides an example for Massachusetts' K–12 spending changes from 1979 to 1989 in real (input-cost-adjusted) terms. The table begins with actual 1979 Massachusetts K–12 spending, reported in real, input-cost-adjusted 1989 dollars, of $4158 per student. Over the course of the decade, Massachusetts' circumstances changed; according to the estimated spending pattern, this would have been expected to raise Massachusetts' spending by $468 + $105 = $573 per pupil in cost-adjusted terms. (Technically, this is computed as $(X_{MA1989} - X_{MA\,1979})\,\hat{\beta}$.) The table shows the change due to the increase in per capita income ($105) separately from the change due to shifts in other circumstances ($468). Massachusetts' spending would also be ex-

---

13 The income effect can be removed from the benchmark for other years using the estimated coefficient for per capita income in each spending area (reported in appendix C) and the difference between Massachusetts' per capita income and the national average for each year (reported in appendix B).

pected to shift along with the general national time trend and shifts in the national average values of political culture variables; over the course of the decade, this would be expected to raise spending in Massachusetts by $894 per pupil. In total, these effects would have been expected to increase Massachusetts' spending by $1467 per pupil if no change had taken place in the relative priority (measured as the divergence between actual and benchmark spending). In fact, however, spending rose over the decade by only $4514 - $4158 = $456 per pupil in real terms, or by $1111 less per student than would have been expected with no change in priority shown toward K–12

Table 2-2

Analysis of 1979–1989 Change in Real Massachusetts Spending Public Elementary and Secondary Education Operating Spending per Enrolled Student

	Spending per enrolled student (1989 dollars)	Percent of 1979 spending
Massachusetts 1979 real spending	4158	100
1979–1989 changes in circumstances		
Change in fiscal need indicators	468	11
Change in per capita income	105	3
General time trend and changes in national choices	894	21
1979–1989 changes in choices	-1111	-27
Massachusetts 1989 real spending	4514	109

education. This $1111 shift constitutes a substantial change in the state's choices concerning how much to emphasize K–12 education.

Interpretation of Statistical Results

In most studies in which statistical regression estimates are presented, the difference between the values estimated and the actual values are interpreted as stemming from random (or at least uncontrolled for) influences. In this study, by contrast, the difference between the benchmark level of spending constructed from the regression results and the actual level of spending is interpreted as a choice made by the state to differ from the standard or reference set of norms created by observing the behavior of the other states. The amount of spending is understood not as determined by a set of influences and an inexplicable random error; instead, it is understood as the outcome of a political process that reflects a set of underlying costs, circumstances, and choices. The statistical process undertaken here attempts to distinguish these influences, none of which is viewed as random.

As a consequence, the usual measures of statistical fit in these equations are an inappropriate indication of the degree to which the equations capture the relevant influences. Generally, when the difference between the actual observed value and the value predicted by an equation is large, we say that the equation does not fit well, that the influences it captures do not explain much of the variation observed, and that the results are therefore relatively unreliable. In this study, the interpretation is quite different. There is no presumption about what fraction of the variation in public spending should be accounted for by the identified public service needs indicators and formal political culture variables; the part of the variation not found to be due to differences in needs and circumstances (as measured by the fiscal circumstance explanatory variables) is ascribed to differences in tastes. A portion of those taste differences is attributed to the political culture measures included in the equations, but the remaining difference is also attributed to (unmeasured) choice differences among the states. If the influences having to do with determinants of need for public services account for only a small proportion of the variation among states, then we have not discovered that the equation is an unreliable predictor; instead, we have determined that there is wide dispersion in relative priorities across states.

This makes it difficult to interpret the usual statistical indicators of goodness of fit and reliability of the estimates, which are based on the classical statistical inference model in which the residual errors are interpreted as random. As a consequence, in this study the best indication of the reliability of the results is their sensitivity to alternative assumptions, to the inclusion of alternative variables, and to different specifications of the relationship between spending and the explanatory variables. As a result, various specifications were used in the development of this study, and where the results vary materially across reasonable alternative specifications mention is made in the text that the results appear to be sensitive to the choice of specification.

Expenditure Data Sources

Reliable data across states and across years is difficult to obtain. By far the best source is U.S. Bureau of the Census data based on all states and a sample of local government units; these data, published each year, give revenues, and both capital and operating expenditures for a variety of areas. They have two major drawbacks. First, they are published rather a long time after the period they cover; the latest data available when this analysis was completed in December 1991 were for fiscal 1989, which for most government units closed in June 1989. Second, they are presented at a rather high level of aggregation; in order to maintain comparability across states, the areas of expenditure in which data are reported are quite broad. For example, the area labeled "public welfare" in the Census data includes both cash assistance programs and Medicaid; for the most recent five years, a reasonable approximation to Medicaid spending can be extracted from figures labelled "vendor payments for medical care," but the separation is not perfect, and no more detailed level of disaggregation is available.

In order to make meaningful comparisons across states, the focus of attention must be on combined spending by state and local governments. There is substantial variety across states in the locus of tax and spending authority for various functions; for example, in some states, nearly all spending on human services is conducted at the state level, while in others, counties and other local governments disburse the bulk of the funds. Moreover, states differ markedly in the degree to which public expenditures are made through the state budget or through independent public authorities. Thus, it is nearly impossible to compare the spending of state government units to each other meaningfully; the comparisons are fraught with complicated adjustments for arbitrary differences in institutional arrangements. *All comparisons in this study are of combined state and local government spending in each area of expenditure unless explicitly noted otherwise.*

The Census data have been published for a number of years, but the further the sample is extended back into the past the greater are the incompatibilities in the data due to changes in definition and classification of spending. The sample period selected for this study is limited to the eleven years from 1979 to 1989, inclusive.

APPENDIX B

Data Sources and Adjustments

The data used in this study were drawn from compilations of data assembled for other purposes, much of it published by the Bureau of the Census. Some of the portions of this section describing the data and its collection are paraphrased from the introduction and appendices to *Government Finances*, published by the Bureau of the Census, and from other descriptions provided with data drawn from other sources.

State and local expenditure data were drawn from the 1979 through 1989 United States Bureau of the Census *Government Finances* annual surveys (table 12 for 1979–1984 and table 22 for 1985–1989). State and local expenditure statistics reported in *Government Finances* are based on annual Census Bureau surveys of state finances and are in current dollars.

Representatives of the Census Bureau compile figures in detail from official records and reports of the various states for most of the data. The Integrated Postsecondary Education Data Survey, conducted annually by the Center for Education Statistics, is the Census Bureau source of state college and university data.

The Census Bureau draws a sample of local governments during the annual Census of Governments consisting of county, municipal, and township governments. Nationwide estimates of local government finance items and totals are based upon summations of state-by-state data; consequently, these estimates are more reliable than the state-area data. Estimates of major United States totals for local governments are subject to a computed sampling variability of less than one-half of 1 percent and other local government totals are generally subject to sampling variability of less than 1 percent. State government finance data are not subject to sampling. Consequently, state-local aggregates used in this report are more reliable than the local government estimates they include.

State and local expenditures for each function include payments from all sources and funds, including amounts spent from borrowing and from previous period balances, as well as from current revenues. Total state and local expenditures for specific functions include any intergovernmental amounts. Intergovernmental "in-kind" aid is not treated as an intergovernmental expenditure. Some transactions between governments have not been isolated in these data. In situations where one government pays a portion of another's retirement system costs, the entire cost of the system is included in the donor government's "current operation" total. Where governments deal with one another as customers and suppliers, the entire transaction is reported with no intergovernmental component.

Expenditures for specific functions do not include any amounts for debt service costs. Interest payments on debt are instead consolidated in an "interest" category. Other transactions not considered as expenditures include payments for debt retirement, extension of loans, purchase of securities, and payment to the federal government of monies withheld for income tax or Social Security purposes.

Spending Areas Used in Study

Total general expenditures include all amounts of money paid out by a government—net of recoveries and other correcting transactions—other than for retirement of debt, investment in securities, extension of credit, or as agency transactions. Expenditures include only external transactions of a government and exclude non-cash transactions such as the provision of perquisites or other payments in kind. Expenditures classified as utilities, liquor stores, employee retirement, and insurance trust are not included in general expenditures. Capital expenditures are included in the total.

Net general expenditures were constructed by subtracting inter-governmental revenue furnished to state and local governments by the federal government for public welfare, elementary and secondary education, and higher education from gross expenditures. Intergovernmental revenue figures were drawn from *Government Finances* (table 5 for 1979–1984 and table 29 for 1985–1989).

Elementary and secondary education expenditures comprise payments for instruction, support services, and other activities of local public schools for kindergarten through high school programs. Not included are direct state expenditures for state educational administration and services, tuition grants, fellowships, aid to private schools, and special programs.

Net elementary and secondary education expenditures were constructed by subtracting intergovernmental revenue furnished to state and local governments by the federal government for elementary and secondary education, and annual current charges levied by state and local governments for such programs, from gross expenditures. Intergovernmental revenue figures for elementary and secondary education are from *Public Education Finances* (table 3 for 1979–1986 and table 9 for 1987–1989) published by the Bureau of the Census. Elementary and secondary education charges were constructed by subtracting "state and local higher education charges" (obtained directly from the Governments Division of the Census Bureau) from "state and local total education charges" (from *Government Finances,* table 5 for 1979–1984 and table 29 for 1985–1989).

Higher education expenditures include payment for activities of institutions operated by the state. Spending on agricultural extension services and experiment stations is not included in this category, nor are expenditures for dormitories, cafeterias, athletic events, bookstores, and other auxiliary activities. Again, direct state expenditures for state educational administration and services, tuition grants, fellowships, aid to private schools, and special programs are not included.

Net higher education expenditures were constructed by subtracting intergovernmental revenue from the federal government to state and local governments for higher education, and annual current charges levied by state and local governments for higher education, from gross expenditures. Intergovernmental revenue figures for higher education were constructed by subtracting revenue for elementary and secondary education from total intergovernmental revenue for education (from *Government Finances,* table 5 for 1979–1984 and table 29 for 1985–1989). "State and local higher education charges" were obtained directly from the Governments Division of the Census Bureau.

Direct assistance expenditures are from the public welfare line item in *Government Finances* and include *cash assistance* paid directly to needy persons under categorical programs (Old Age Assistance, Aid to Families with Dependent Children, Aid to the Blind, and Aid to the Disabled) and any other welfare programs; *vendor payments* made directly to private purveyors for medical care, burials, and other welfare-related commodities; costs of provision and operation by the government of *welfare institutions; payments to other governments* for welfare purposes; *administrative costs;* and support for *private welfare agencies* and other services. Most Medicaid costs are included in vendor payments.

Net direct assistance expenditures were constructed by subtracting intergovernmental revenue from the federal government to state and local governments for public welfare programs from gross expenditures. Intergovernmental revenue figures for public welfare were drawn from *Government Finances,* table 5 for 1979–1984 and table 29 for 1985–1989.

Health and hospitals expenditures are a combination of the "health" and "hospital" line items in *Government Finances.* The health portion includes public health administration; research and education; categorical health programs; treatment and immunization clinics; nursing; environmental health activities such as air and water pollution control; ambulance service, if provided separately from fire protection services; and other general public health activities such as school health services provided by state health agencies and mosquito abatement. The hospital portion includes financing, construction, acquisition, maintenance or operation of hospital facilities, provision of hospital care, and support of public or private hospitals. Expenditures for health and hospital services provided to welfare recipients are reported as vendor payments under public welfare expenditures.

Net health and hospital expenditures were constructed by subtracting annual current charges levied by state and local governments from total health and hospital expenditures. The source of hospital charges data is *Government Finances,* table 5 for 1979–1984 and table 29 for 1985–1989.

Highway expenditures include payments for the construction, maintenance, and operation of highways, streets, and related structures, including toll highways, bridges, tunnels, ferries, street lighting, and snow and ice removal. Highway policing and traffic control expenditures are not included.

Public safety expenditures used in this study are the sum of the police, fire, and protective inspection and regulation expenditure categories.

- Police protection includes police patrols and communications, crime prevention activities, detention and custody of persons awaiting trial, traffic safety, and vehicular inspection. Payments for police and traffic safety activities make up the bulk of local police protection expenditures. State expenditures are primarily for highway police activities.

- Fire protection includes fire fighting organization and auxiliary services, fire inspection and investigation, support of volunteer fire forces, and other fire prevention activities. Fire hydrants, water, and other facilities provided by other agencies of government are included.

- Protective inspection and regulation includes spending on the regulation of private enterprise for the protection of the public and inspection of hazardous activities except for major functions, such as fire prevention, health, and natural resources. Licensing activities and collections are not included.

Corrections expenditures include spending for confinement and correction of adults and minors convicted of offenses against the law, and pardon, probation, and parole activities.

Operating expenditures were compiled by subtracting capital outlays (from *Government Finances,* table 14 for 1978–1984 and table 24 for 1985–1989) from specific gross expenditure functions. This study compiled operating expenditures for total general expenditures, elementary and secondary education, higher education, health and hospitals, and highways. These figures are available for 1979 through 1989.

Adjustments to Expenditure Data

Each expenditure is divided by an input-cost index, which varies both by state and by year (National Average 1989 = 1.00). The input-cost index for non-direct assistance expenditures is a weighted average of the state's unit labor cost index and a state CPI. Direct assistance expenditures were adjusted by a weighted average of unit labor costs, the state CPI, and a state health services cost index.

The weights for the states' labor cost index (w_l) is the U.S. average ratio of employment costs to total direct general expenditures for the function, derived by Robert Rafuse.[1] The input-cost index for non-direct assistance expenditures equals

$$w_l * (wage\ index) + (1-w_l) * CPI$$

---

1   Robert W. Rafuse, Jr., *Representative Expenditures: Addressing the Neglected Dimension of Fiscal Capacity,* Advisory Commission on Intergovernmental Relations, Washington, DC, December 1990.

Following are the Rafuse labor ratios (w_l):

General Expenditures	.495
Primary & Secondary Education	.753
Higher Education	.675
Direct Assistance	.128
Health & Hospitals	.616
Highways	.287
Police	.895
Fire	.867
Corrections	.672

The weight for the health services cost index for direct assistance (w_m) is the 1988 proportion of "vendor payments for medical care" to "total public welfare expenditures" by state. The input-cost index for direct assistance expenditures equals:

$$w_l*(wage\ index)+w_m*\ (health\ services\ cost\ index)+(1-w_l-w_m)*CPI$$

Functions for which operating expenditures alone were available were also adjusted by an input-cost index. Those functions include total general expenditures, elementary and secondary education, higher education, health and hospitals, and highway expenditures. Since a larger proportion of a function's operating expenditures are labor-related, the Rafuse labor ratios were multiplied by the ratio of the function's total expenditures to its operating expenditures in 1988. The formulas for each function's input cost index remain the same, using the new labor ratios as weights for the labor cost index.

Unit Labor Cost Index

The unit labor cost index with National Average 1989 = 1.00 was created in two steps. First, an annual average wage for private sector employment in each state was constructed by taking a weighted average of each state's average annual pay for 6 major industries: construction; manufacturing; transportation and public utilities; wholesale trade; finance, insurance and real estate; and services. The source of these data is the "Average Annual Pay by State and Industry" tables of the *News* bulletin published by the Bureau of Labor Statistics, United States Department of Labor, Washington, DC. Data are available for 1979–1989. The weights for these figures are the percent of the U.S. private labor force employed annually in each of the industries named above. The source of the employment data is "Table 63. Employees on Nonagricultural Payrolls by Major Industry and Manufacturing Group," from *Employment and Earnings,* U.S. Department of Labor Statistics, January 1990. Annual data are available for 1979–1989. Second, each state's annual private sector wage was then divided by the 1989 national average wage to create the unit labor cost index with National Average 1989 = 1.00.

Cost-of-Living Index

A state cost-of-living index (CPI) with National Average 1989 = 1.00 was constructed in three steps. First an annual CPI for selected metropolitan areas (msas), 4 overall regions and 4 non-metropolitan regions were constructed with urban United States = 1.00 for each year (i.e., 1979 urban U.S. = 1.00, 1980 urban U.S. = 1.00, etc.). These indexes were then adjusted so that only 1989 urban U.S. = 1.00. Finally, a state CPI was constructed as a population-weighted average of the msa and regional CPIs.

The annual CPI for each msa was based on the 1981 Urban family budgets, which shows the relative cost of living in 25 metropolitan statistical areas and in the non-metropolitan areas of four regions, with U.S. urban average cost = 100. The source of this data is the total consumption figure in "Table 5. Indexes of comparative costs based on an intermediate budget for a 4-person family" from *Urban Family Budgets and Comparative Indexes for Selected Urban Areas,* Bureau of Labor Statistics, U.S. Department of Labor, Autumn 1981. A regional metropolitan figure was constructed by taking the population-weighted average of the individual msa figures in each of the four regions. Autumn 1981 was the last release of this data.

Annual growth rates of the msa and regional CPIs were then applied successively (and regressively) to the 1981 family budget. Sources of the growth rates are the "All items" component of "Table 17A. Consumer Price Index for All Urban Consumers: Selected Areas," "Table 12A. Consumer Price Index for All Urban Consumers: Regions" and "Table 14A. Consumer Price Index for All Urban Consumers: Cross classification of region and population sizes," *CPI Detailed Report,* U.S. Department of Labor, Bureau of Labor Statistics. These data are available annually in January (although table numbers vary from year to year). The 11-year series were converted so that National Average 1989 = 1.00.

A cost-of-living index for each state for each year was then constructed by taking a weighted average of the CPIs of the component msas, the overall urban regions and the regions of "size class D" (which corresponds to areas of fewer than 50,000 people). The msa's own index was used for the proportion of the state's population in that specific metropolitan area. The regional CPI index was used for the remaining metropolitan population, and the "size class D" CPI index was used for the non-metropolitan population. The source of the urban population data is the *Statistical Abstract of the United States - 1988,* Appendix II, "Metropolitan Statistical Areas and their Components," June 30, 1987. State population figures are also from the *Statistical Abstract of the United States.*

For example, 54.5% of Minnesota's population is in the Minneapolis-St. Paul msa, 12.3% of its population is in msas for which no urban budget figures were available, and 33.2% of its population is in nonmetropolitan areas. With the 1981 Minneapolis msa index equal to 97, the North Central metropolitan index equal to 100.22, and the North Central nonmetropolitan index equal to 93, Minnesota's 1981 CPI (with National Average 1981 = 100) equals

$$.545*(97) + .123*(100.22) + .332*(93) = 96.01$$

To get a 1981 index value for Minnesota based on a 1989 national average of 100, that figure was then divided by the ratio of the 1989 national average to the 1981 national average (1.364), giving a 1981 index for Minnesota of 70.4.

Health Services Cost Index

Although several possible indexes for health services costs were considered to deflate the Medicaid portion of direct assistance expenditures, each index was substantially flawed in showing regional price differences by state over time.[2] Under the Health Care Finance Administration's Prospective Payment System, which compensates hospitals for their inpatient treatment of Medicare beneficiaries, the labor-related proportion of costs is considered to be approximately 75 percent. We thus created a health services cost index equal to

$$.75*(wage\ index) + .25*CPI.$$

Sources of Demographic and Characteristic Data

Population (POP89) figures were drawn from the "State Rankings" table, for 1989 figures, and the "Population" table for 1983–1988 figures in the *Statistical Abstract of the United States, 1990,* Bureau of the Census, U.S. Department of Commerce. Figures for 1980–1982 were from the "Resident Population - States: 1970 to 1982" table from the *Statistical Abstract of the United States, 1984.* Figures for 1979 were from the *Statistical Abstract, 1986.* Figures are in thousands.

---

2 Examples of indexes considered were the medical CPI, the HCFA hospital wage index, an index based on hospital room charges, and an index based on per capita health spending by state estimated by Lewin/ICF and published by the Families USA Foundation, 1990. The major flaws in the above indexes were either 1) failure to separate changes in costs versus changes in the "market basket" of services, 2) using list prices versus actual prices of certain services, or 3) lack of annual data.

Personal income per capita (CAPINCA) for 1979 through 1989 is derived from total personal income in current dollars from "Table 1. Total and Per Capita Personal Income by States and Regions," *Survey of Current Business*, August 1990, U.S. Bureau of Economic Analysis. Income figures are divided by the states' population figures and are adjusted by the states' CPI. Figures are in 1989 constant dollars, in thousands.

Percent of population poor (POVP89A) is the number of people in a state who have incomes below the poverty level determined by the Social Security Administration's poverty index, divided by the state's total population. The poverty index is based solely on money income and does not reflect the fact that many low-income persons receive non-cash benefits. The 1979 index is based on the Department of Agriculture's 1961 economy food plan and consumption requirements. The poverty index was revised by federal interagency committees in 1980.

Since poverty rates for states are not published annually, we used two sources of unadjusted poverty data: *1980 Census of Population* for 1979 (published in the *Statistical Abstract of the United States, 1989*, Table 733) and the Institute for Research on Poverty of the University of Wisconsin - Madison for the mid-1980s (published in its newsletter *Focus*, Fall 1988) and the late 1980s (*Focus*, Spring 1991).

The mid-1980s series of poverty rates for persons by state was created by the Institute for Research on Poverty by pooling data from the March 1985, 1986, and 1987 Current Population Survey (CPS) data tapes; a late-1980s series was created pooling 1987, 1988, and 1989 CPS files. We used the mid-1980s series for 1985 and the late-1980s series for 1987, 1988, and 1989. Our nominal poverty figures for 1980 through 1984 were created by interpolating between the 1979 and 1985 numbers. For 1986 an average of the 1985 and 1987 rates was used.

Since the poverty rates do not reflect differences in costs of living between states, we adjusted the series to do so. All of the nominal poverty series were multiplied by a ratio that reflects regional cost of living differences. The ratio was constructed as follows: using each state's income distribution for a family of four in the late 1980s (obtained from *Focus,* Spring 1991), we determined at which percentile the national poverty income for a family of four ($12,092) fell in each state. Given the difference in each state's cost of living, we calculated the "real" poverty income for a family of four by multiplying the national poverty income level by each state's cost of living index. We then determined the percentile at which the real poverty income fell on each state's income distribution. The ratio of the real to nominal poverty percentiles was multiplied by the individual poverty rate in each state to obtain adjusted poverty rates.

To illustrate, in the late 1980s 12.10% of Massachusetts families of four had incomes at or below the national poverty level of $12,092. With the cost of living in the state 1.14 times the national average in 1989, the real poverty income for a family of four was $13,836; 14.48% of the state's families of four were below this income. The state's real poverty rate in 1989 is then calculated by multiplying its nominal rate of 8.9% by 1.197 (the ratio of 14.48% to 12.10%), and equaled 10.65%.

Percent of population elderly (ELDPCT) is the total number of persons in each state older than 65 years, divided by the state's total population. The total numbers of persons older than 65 were drawn from tables 35 (1979), 32 (1980), 33 (1981), 34 (1982), 29 (1984), 26 (1986), 27 (1987), and 28 (1988) in the *Statistical Abstract.* The source of these data is *Current Population Reports,* U.S. Bureau of the Census. The missing years were constructed by interpolating between the years for which figures were available. The 1988 figure was used for 1989.

Percent of population young (YNGPCT) is the total number of persons in each state younger than 18 years, divided by the state's total population. The total numbers of persons younger than 18 were drawn from tables 35 (1979), 32 (1980), 33 (1981), 34 (1982), 29 (1984), 26 (1986), 27 (1987), and 28 (1988) in the *Statistical*

Abstract. The source of these data is *Current Population Reports,* U.S. Bureau of the Census. The missing years were constructed by interpolating between the years for which figures were available. The 1988 figure was used for 1989.

Proportion of elderly to poor population (ELDPOORA) is derived by dividing the percent of population elderly (ELDPCT) by the percent of population poor (POVP89A).

Proportion of young to poor population (YNGPOORA) is derived by dividing the percent of population young (YNGPCT) by the percent of population poor (POVP89A).

Proportion of female-headed households to poor population (FEMHPOOR) is derived by dividing the number of female-headed households by the number of poor people. The source for the number of female-headed households is *State Demographics: Population Profiles of 50 States,* prepared by the American Demographics Magazine, edited by Business1-Irwin, Homewood, IL 60430. The 1989 data are from "Table 1. Selected Population and Housing Characteristics" for each state, CPH-1 Reports: 1990, published by the Statistical Information Office, Bureau of the Census, Washington, DC. The original sources of the data are 1980 and 1990 U.S. Censuses, respectively. Household data for intermediate years were interpolated from the 1979 and 1989 figures. The annual number of poor people was constructed by multiplying the poverty percentage by the state's population.

Percent of population enrolled in public elementary and secondary schools (ELSCHPCT) is the total number of children enrolled in public elementary and secondary schools by state, divided by the state's total population. The source of school enrollment data is "Table 37. Enrollment in Public Elementary and Secondary Schools, by level and State" in the *Digest of Education Statistics, 1989,* National Center for Education Statistics, U.S. Department of Education. Annual data are available for 1979 through 1989.

Percent of population enrolled in public institutions of higher education (HIEDPCT) is the total number of full-time equivalent

(FTE) enrollments in public institutions of higher education divided by the state's total population. FTEs are all credit and non-credit program enrollments, including summer session students. The source of these data is "Table 5. The Basic Data, Historical" in *State Profiles: Financing Public Higher Education,* annual, published by Research Associates of Washington, Washington, DC. Annual data are available for 1979 through 1989.

Percent of population living in metropolitan areas (METPCT), is the percent of the state's total population that live in one of the 262 metropolitan statistical areas as defined by the U.S. Office of Management and Budget. The data are from tables 26 (1978), 19 (1980), 22 (1981), 23 (1984), 33 (1986), and 35 (1987 and 1988) of the *Statistical Abstract of the United States.* The source of these data is the *1980 Census of Population, Supplementary Report, Metropolitan Statistical Areas,* updated in *Current Population Reports,* U.S. Bureau of the Census. The missing years were constructed by interpolating between the years for which figures were available. The 1988 figure was used for 1989.

Heating degree days (HEATDD) is the difference between the average temperature each day and 65°, summed over the days in which the average temperature fell below 65°. Data are from "Table 373. Normal Monthly and Seasonal Heating Degree Days, 65° Base - Selected Cities," based on a standard 30-year period, 1951 through 1980, in the *Statistical Abstract of the United States, 1990.* Cities from all fifty states are represented. For those states with more than one city listed, the heating degree days were calculated as a weighted average of the cities, with weights based on the cities' populations.

Crime rates (CRIMRAT9) is the rate of violent and property crimes committed in each state for 1979–1989. Data are from "Table 3. Index of Crime: Region, Geographic Division and State," *Crime in the United States,* annual, U.S. Department of Justice, FBI. Annual figures are available for 1979 through 1989.

Motor vehicles per capita (MOTOPOP) is the number of registered motor vehicles divided by the population in each state. The source of the motor vehicle data is the "Motor-Vehicle Registrations and Vehicle-Miles of Travel, by State" table in *Highway Statistics,* annual, U.S. Department of Transportation, Federal Highway Administration. Annual figures are available for 1979 through 1989.

Miles of highway per vehicle (MILPVEH) is the state's total number of highway miles divided by the number of registered motor vehicles. The source of the highway miles data is "Table 1020. Highway Mileage - Urban, Rural, and Federal-Aid Highway System: 1987," *Statistical Abstract of the United States, 1990.* The 1987 number of highway miles was used for every year, while the annual number of registered motor vehicles was used for each year.

Land area per vehicle (AREAVEH) is the number of square miles of land area in the state divided by the number of registered motor vehicles. The source of land area data is "Table 337. Area of States and Other Areas: 1980," *Statistical Abstract of the United States, 1990.* Separate vehicle numbers were gathered for each year from 1979 to 1989.

Sources of Political Culture Data

Political culture (PC and PCSQ) is a score developed by Ira Sharkansky, based on the work of Daniel Elazar, which attempts to measure a state's overall political orientation in terms of its viewing the political order primarily as "individualistic" (which emphasizes the democratic order as a marketplace), "moralistic" (which emphasizes a commonwealth conception of the political order), or "traditionalistic" (which is rooted in a paternalistic and elitist conception of the commonwealth). The scale, which does not change over time, is as follows, with the first letter in each pairing denoting a primary culture:

M	MT	MI	IM	I	IT	TI	TM	T
1	2	3	4	5	6	7	8	9

The designations form a continuum on at least three political dimensions: the degree of political participation, the size and perquisites of the government bureaucracy, and the scope, magnitude or costs of government programs—with lower numbers corresponding to more of the political dimensions cited above. Data are taken from "Table 1. Each State's Score on the Political Culture Scale" in Ira Sharkansky's "The Utility of Elazar's Political Culture" (*Polity,* Vol. II, Fall 1969, pp. 66–83), which in turn was based largely on the work of Daniel Elazar in *American Federalism: A View From the States* (New York: Thomas Y. Crowell, 1966). Since Sharkansky gives no political culture score for Hawaii, we used the national average (excluding Alaska) for that state.

Party of the governor (GOVS) is a dummy variable representing the party of each state's governor in each calendar year from 1979 through 1989. Democratic governors were assigned a value of 1, and all other gubernatorial parties (mainly Republican) were assigned a value of 0. Data on the party of each state's governor were obtained from "Vote Cast for and Governor Elected, by State," (table 433 for 1983–1989 and table 819 for 1979–1982) in *Statistical Abstract of the United States, 1990 and 1986,* respectively, published by the U.S. Bureau of the Census. The source of data used for each of these tables was *America Votes,* the Elections Research Center, Washington, DC, biennial and unpublished data.

Formal powers of the governor (GOVPOW) is an index created by Thad Beyle, ranging from 4 to 32, measuring gubernatorial tenure potential, appointment power, veto power, political strength in the legislature, budget-making power, and legislative budget-changing power, as found in the state's laws. Beyle scored states along each of these dimensions, and summed the individual scores to produce the combined index, which is fixed over the study period. The index is published in "Table 6.7. Combined Index of the Formal Powers of the Governors, 1989," appendix B and discussed in chapter 6, "Governors,"of *Politics in the American States,* Gray et al., p. 574.

Proportion of Democrats in both houses combined (COMBDEM) is the number of Democrats in the upper and lower houses of each state legislature divided by the total number of legislators. Data are annual for 1979–1989 and are from "Composition of State Legislatures, by Political Party Affiliation" (table 434 for 1983–1989 and table 820 for 1979–1982) in *Statistical Abstract of the United States, 1990 and 1986,* respectively. The sources of data used for each of these tables was the Council of State Governments, Lexington, KY, 1982–1984, *Book of the States,* biennial; beginning 1986, *State Elective Officials and the Legislatures,* biennial. Since no such data is available for Nebraska, whose legislature is elected without party designation, the national average proportion (excluding Alaska) was used.

Proportion of women in both houses of the legislature combined (FEMTOT), is the number of female legislators divided by the total legislators in each state. Data are annual for 1979 through 1989, and are from "Women in State Legislatures," fact sheet, Center for the American Woman and Politics, Eagleton Institute of Politics (New Brunswick, NJ: Rutgers University, 1979–1989).

Liberal quotient (NEWLQ) for each state was constructed from a score created by the Americans for Democratic Action (ADA), which measures the degree to which each Senator and Representative's voting record is "liberal" or "conservative," based on select votes in Congress on judicial, social, economic, foreign, and military policy. Scores range from 0 to 100, with higher scores referring to "more liberal." The liberal quotient for each state was constructed by averaging the liberal quotients of its congressional delegation. Data are annual for 1979–1989 and are from the ADA "Voting Record," found in *ADA Today* and *ADA World* (Washington, DC: Americans for Democratic Action, 1979–1989).

Regions (REGNE, REGMA, REGENC, REGWNC, REGSA, REGESC, REGWSC, REGMT, REGPAC) are nine dummy variables, which do not vary over time, representing the nine Census divisions in the United States. In "REGNE" states in New England were assigned a value of 1 each year; all others were assigned a value of 0. Similar dummy variables were created for the remaining regions of Middle Atlantic, East North Central, West North Central, South Atlantic, East South Central, West South Central, Mountain, and Pacific. Definitions of each census division are found in the "State Rankings" table of the *Statistical Abstract of the United States, 1989.*

Table B-1
Index to Data Series
Variable Description

Dependent (Adjusted Expenditures, in dollars)

CAPEXP	Total general expenditures per capita
NETGENEX	General expenditures per capita net federal reimbursements for elementary, secondary, and higher education, and direct assistance
CAPEXPOP	Total general operating expenditures per capita
WELPOOR	Total direct assistance expenditures per poor person
WELPOORN	Direct assistance expenditures per poor person net federal reimbursements for direct assistance
NETHHOS	Health and hospital expenditures per capita net state charges for health and hospital services
HHOPCAP	Health and hospital operating expenditures per capita
SAFECAP	Total public safety expenditures per capita
CORRECAP	Total corrections expenditures per capita
NETELED	Elementary and secondary education expenditures per pupil net federal reimbursements and state charges for elementary and secondary education services
OPELED	Elementary and secondary education operating expenditures per pupil
NETHIED	Higher education expenditures per pupil net federal reimbursements and state charges for higher education services
OPHIED	Higher education operating expenditures per pupil
HWTOCAR	Total highway expenditures per registered motor vehicle
HWOPCAR	Highway operating expenditures per registered motor vehicle

Independent (Characteristics)

POVP89A	Percent of population poor
METPCT	Percent of population living in metropolitan areas
ELDPCT	Percent of population elderly
YNGPCT	Percent of population young

Table B-1 (continued)

HEATDD	Heating degree days
CRIMRAT9	State crime rate per capita
MILPVEH	Miles of highway per registered motor vehicle
CAPINCA	Per capita income (in thousands of dollars)
HIEDPCT	Percent of population enrolled in public institutions of higher education
ELSCHPCT	Percent of population enrolled in public elementary and secondary schools
FEMHPOOR	Number of female-headed households per thousand poor persons
ELDPOORA	Proportion of elderly to poor population
YNGPOORA	Proportion of young to poor population
MOTOPOP	Registered motor vehicles per capita
AREAVEH	State land area (in square miles) per registered motor vehicle

Independent (Political Culture)

NEWLQ	Liberal quotient (0–100)
PC	Political culture
PCSQ	Political culture squared
COMBDEM	Percent of legislature Democrats, both houses combined
GOVS	Political party of governor (1=Democrat; 0=Republican)
GOVPOW	Formal powers of governor
FEMTOT	Percent of female legislators

Table B-2

Sample Statistics on Data Series (1989)

VARIABLE	OBS	MEAN	STD ERROR	MINIMUM	MAXIMUM
Dependent (Adjusted Expenditures)					
CAPEXP	49	3115.5	446.71	2452.8	5121.5
NETGENEX	49	2806.1	430.36	2120.6	4836.0
CAPEXPOP	49	2707.8	393.07	2137.4	4349.1
WELPOOR	49	3017.4	1351.0	1113.0	7161.9
WELPOORN	49	1317.0	853.81	155.24	3672.4
NETHHOS	49	143.68	41.366	73.262	315.57
HHOPCAP	49	255.42	95.428	117.37	555.71
SAFECAP	49	171.85	42.859	81.281	319.91
CORRECAP	49	73.891	25.614	28.312	154.97
NETELED	49	4226.5	798.71	2772.6	6238.4
OPELED	49	4327.7	785.09	2924.5	6455.6
NETHIED	49	4549.5	1406.1	977.64	8198.2
OPHIED	49	9289.0	1771.6	6174.9	15050.
HWTOCAR	49	354.80	84.698	179.64	623.05
HWOPCAR	49	155.79	46.122	84.646	285.43
Independent (Characteristics)					
POVP89A	49	0.12911	0.36996E-01	0.52349E-01	0.22939
METPCT	49	0.64259	0.21960	0.20000	1.0000
ELDPCT	49	0.12355	0.17455E-01	0.84000E-01	0.17800
YNGPCT	49	0.26392	0.24308E-01	0.22600	0.37300
HEATDD	49	4951.1	2126.2	0.00000	9075.0
CRIMRAT9	49	0.50789E-01	0.14066E-01	0.23628E-01	0.88045E-01
MILPVEH	49	0.32750E-01	0.27729E-01	0.55299E-02	0.13560
CAPINCA	49	16.727	2.1557	13.068	22.095
HIEDPCT	49	0.30498E-01	0.63624E-02	0.18987E-01	0.47079E-01
ELSCHPCT	49	0.16801	0.21194E-01	0.13527	0.25483
FEMHPOOR	49	331.29	96.982	200.20	605.69
ELDPOORA	49	1.0357	0.33769	0.51908	2.1586
YNGPOORA	49	2.1946	0.63226	1.2991	4.8330
MOTOPOP	49	0.78794	0.10563	0.55827	1.0253
AREAVEH	49	0.34283E-01	0.46399E-01	0.13817E-02	0.20084
Independent (Political Culture)					
NEWLQ	49	47.024	18.838	5.0000	89.615
PC	49	4.8832	2.6493	0.49746	9.0000
PCSQ	49	30.721	27.631	0.24746	81.000
COMBDEM	49	0.60452	0.15695	0.29953	0.89655
GOVS	49	0.55102	0.50254	0.00000	1.0000
GOVPOW	49	22.000	2.8211	15.000	29.000
FEMTOT	49	0.16824	0.75639E-01	0.20833E-01	0.32075

Table B-3

Sample Statistics on Data Series (1988)

VARIABLE	OBS	MEAN	STD ERROR	MINIMUM	MAXIMUM
Dependent (Adjusted Expenditures)					
CAPEXP	49	3012.0	461.59	2376.5	5260.4
NETGENEX	49	2716.6	445.94	2085.4	4973.7
CAPEXPOP	49	2611.1	394.37	2048.5	4334.7
WELPOOR	49	2848.8	1301.1	1007.4	6977.3
WELPOORN	49	1219.1	796.88	148.71	3536.8
NETHHOS	49	139.28	43.699	71.638	302.46
HHOPCAP	49	241.19	93.081	117.21	586.86
SAFECAP	49	167.10	42.897	79.614	301.94
CORRECAP	49	67.978	26.241	27.087	173.93
NETELED	49	4050.1	771.68	2526.3	6508.8
OPELED	49	4161.6	759.50	2843.2	6375.3
NETHIED	49	4575.6	1274.9	922.98	8259.6
OPHIED	49	9091.9	1673.4	5862.3	14750.
HWTOCAR	49	352.83	82.121	194.10	642.21
HWOPCAR	49	150.26	39.965	82.376	246.97
Independent (Characteristics)					
POVP89A	49	0.12952	0.37233E-01	0.52187E-01	0.23025
METPCT	49	0.64259	0.21960	0.20000	1.0000
ELDPCT	49	0.12355	0.17455E-01	0.84000E-01	0.17800
YNGPCT	49	0.26392	0.24308E-01	0.22600	0.37300
HEATDD	49	4951.1	2126.2	0.00000	9075.0
CRIMRAT9	49	0.50278E-01	0.14253E-01	0.22390E-01	0.89380E-01
MILPVEH	49	0.33062E-01	0.27766E-01	0.57812E-02	0.13167
CAPINCA	49	16.385	2.1738	12.841	21.845
HIEDPCT	49	0.29887E-01	0.62036E-02	0.18254E-01	0.45490E-01
ELSCHPCT	49	0.16939	0.21131E-01	0.13467	0.25192
FEMHPOOR	49	326.31	97.664	195.60	598.67
ELDPOORA	49	1.0332	0.33893	0.51703	2.1653
YNGPOORA	49	2.1887	0.63303	1.2942	4.8480
MOTOPOP	49	0.78444	0.10270	0.54967	1.0234
AREAVEH	49	0.34811E-01	0.47256E-01	0.13571E-02	0.20338
Independent (Political Culture)					
NEWLQ	49	49.852	20.564	5.0000	91.154
PC	49	4.8832	2.6493	0.49746	9.0000
PCSQ	49	30.721	27.631	0.24746	81.000
COMBDEM	49	0.60008	0.16450	0.28571	0.90370
GOVS	49	0.51020	0.50508	0.00000	1.0000
GOVPOW	49	22.000	2.8211	15.000	29.000
FEMTOT	49	0.15374	0.67670E-01	0.27778E-01	0.32547

Table B-4

Sample Statistics on Data Series (1987)

VARIABLE	OBS	MEAN	STD ERROR	MINIMUM	MAXIMUM
Dependent (Adjusted Expenditures)					
CAPEXP	49	2981.7	501.13	2372.9	5493.2
NETGENEX	49	2694.7	487.19	2149.3	5244.2
CAPEXPOP	49	2585.2	423.03	2033.9	4557.3
WELPOOR	49	2838.9	1363.8	963.33	7163.2
WELPOORN	49	1252.5	831.14	153.85	3691.1
NETHHOS	49	134.46	42.865	78.625	296.80
HHOPCAP	49	236.70	92.700	115.92	604.26
SAFECAP	49	164.87	42.939	84.850	305.51
CORRECAP	49	64.113	23.355	25.889	138.14
NETELED	49	3931.7	803.79	2359.1	7123.2
OPELED	49	4043.3	781.26	2765.5	6808.3
NETHIED	49	4971.8	1581.7	1640.8	10726.
OPHIED	49	9319.1	1751.9	6020.0	14041.
HWTOCAR	49	362.00	106.33	198.68	806.67
HWOPCAR	49	168.49	53.198	88.611	338.48
Independent (Characteristics)					
POVP89A	49	0.12994	0.37599E-01	0.51702E-01	0.23170
METPCT	49	0.64110	0.22028	0.19600	1.0000
ELDPCT	49	0.12259	0.17940E-01	0.82000E-01	0.17800
YNGPCT	49	0.26569	0.24538E-01	0.22500	0.37400
HEATDD	49	4951.1	2126.2	0.00000	9075.0
CRIMRAT9	49	0.49990E-01	0.13520E-01	0.21910E-01	0.85030E-01
MILPVEH	49	0.33791E-01	0.28094E-01	0.58986E-02	0.13268
CAPINCA	49	15.997	2.0421	12.352	21.087
HIEDPCT	49	0.29587E-01	0.62080E-02	0.18029E-01	0.45276E-01
ELSCHPCT	49	0.17021	0.20362E-01	0.13590	0.25179
FEMHPOOR	49	322.09	100.93	190.63	609.58
ELDPOORA	49	1.0246	0.34747	0.50107	2.2243
YNGPOORA	49	2.1975	0.63385	1.3026	4.8548
MOTOPOP	49	0.77101	0.10495	0.53787	0.97551
AREAVEH	49	0.35426E-01	0.47998E-01	0.14107E-02	0.21158
Independent (Political Culture)					
NEWLQ	49	50.092	20.133	4.6667	90.667
PC	49	4.8832	2.6493	0.49746	9.0000
PCSQ	49	30.721	27.631	0.24746	81.000
COMBDEM	49	0.60016	0.16491	0.28571	0.90805
GOVS	49	0.51020	0.50508	0.00000	1.0000
GOVPOW	49	22.000	2.8211	15.000	29.000
FEMTOT	49	0.15288	0.68897E-01	0.22989E-01	0.32547

Table B-5

Sample Statistics on Data Series (1986)

VARIABLE	OBS	MEAN	STD ERROR	MINIMUM	MAXIMUM
Dependent (Adjusted Expenditures)					
CAPEXP	49	2916.7	524.05	2276.7	5652.5
NETGENEX	49	2633.1	514.58	2061.6	5429.6
CAPEXPOP	49	2533.0	416.90	1956.7	4459.2
WELPOOR	49	2605.8	1207.1	1044.8	5617.0
WELPOORN	49	1121.4	706.47	235.25	2809.2
NETHHOS	49	132.35	36.482	71.148	280.11
HHOPCAP	49	234.96	87.610	114.64	554.56
SAFECAP	49	161.52	41.129	85.171	307.25
CORRECAP	49	61.546	21.975	23.128	129.27
NETELED	49	3817.0	802.96	2484.5	7416.4
OPELED	49	3960.8	769.05	2719.7	6976.3
NETHIED	49	4932.9	1739.6	1299.6	12253.
OPHIED	49	9335.3	1712.2	6239.5	14397.
HWTOCAR	49	372.50	130.21	186.47	990.24
HWOPCAR	49	168.37	53.570	84.140	322.20
Independent (Characteristics)					
POVP89A	49	0.13395	0.35752E-01	0.57273E-01	0.23226
METPCT	49	0.63890	0.22084	0.19400	1.0000
ELDPCT	49	0.12063	0.18207E-01	0.80000E-01	0.17700
YNGPCT	49	0.26745	0.24506E-01	0.22500	0.37200
HEATDD	49	4951.1	2126.2	0.00000	9075.0
CRIMRAT9	49	0.49251E-01	0.13829E-01	0.23167E-01	0.82284E-01
MILPVEH	49	0.34457E-01	0.28955E-01	0.59071E-02	0.13309
CAPINCA	49	15.679	1.9105	12.021	20.195
HIEDPCT	49	0.29646E-01	0.61729E-02	0.18340E-01	0.45862E-01
ELSCHPCT	49	0.17052	0.19715E-01	0.13742	0.25000
FEMHPOOR	49	304.86	92.534	180.24	585.28
ELDPOORA	49	0.96524	0.30664	0.48738	2.0254
YNGPOORA	49	2.1197	0.55244	1.2847	4.4174
MOTOPOP	49	0.76545	0.10457	0.53470	1.0428
AREAVEH	49	0.36519E-01	0.50447E-01	0.14785E-02	0.22229
Independent (Political Culture)					
NEWLQ	49	43.299	21.599	2.0000	88.333
PC	49	4.8832	2.6493	0.49746	9.0000
PCSQ	49	30.721	27.631	0.24746	81.000
COMBDEM	49	0.57957	0.18588	0.19231	0.90805
GOVS	49	0.67347	0.47380	0.00000	1.0000
GOVPOW	49	22.000	2.8211	15.000	29.000
FEMTOT	49	0.14367	0.65803E-01	0.22989E-01	0.33019

Table B-6

Sample Statistics on Data Series (1985)

VARIABLE	OBS	MEAN	STD ERROR	MINIMUM	MAXIMUM
Dependent (Adjusted Expenditures)					
CAPEXP	49	2782.5	514.86	2150.8	5331.8
NETGENEX	49	2510.4	505.26	1922.0	5133.3
CAPEXPOP	49	2419.0	394.34	1869.6	4089.3
WELPOOR	49	2398.1	1086.0	1064.3	4631.7
WELPOORN	49	1027.6	623.15	213.99	2440.4
NETHHOS	49	125.63	33.804	81.638	273.86
HHOPCAP	49	228.13	78.981	107.78	481.27
SAFECAP	49	157.28	39.339	90.160	288.87
CORRECAP	49	56.894	18.769	23.868	108.49
NETELED	49	3629.1	780.51	2426.5	7108.4
OPELED	49	3791.7	742.66	2632.5	6551.5
NETHIED	49	4497.0	1541.0	-691.21	8946.1
OPHIED	49	8788.3	1526.6	5698.4	14274.
HWTOCAR	49	362.64	118.69	192.96	855.07
HWOPCAR	49	167.72	51.593	71.831	319.75
Independent (Characteristics)					
POVP89A	49	0.13799	0.34848E-01	0.62330E-01	0.23287
METPCT	49	0.63723	0.22159	0.19150	1.0000
ELDPCT	49	0.11920	0.18292E-01	0.78500E-01	0.17650
YNGPCT	49	0.26991	0.24921E-01	0.22700	0.37550
HEATDD	49	4951.1	2126.2	0.00000	9075.0
CRIMRAT9	49	0.47298E-01	0.12962E-01	0.22530E-01	0.75740E-01
MILPVEH	49	0.34962E-01	0.28795E-01	0.62519E-02	0.13167
CAPINCA	49	15.181	1.8195	11.637	19.413
HIEDPCT	49	0.30126E-01	0.61896E-02	0.19174E-01	0.45416E-01
ELSCHPCT	49	0.17053	0.18983E-01	0.13744	0.24498
FEMHPOOR	49	290.34	88.431	163.32	577.60
ELDPOORA	49	0.91849	0.27834	0.47784	1.8691
YNGPOORA	49	2.0644	0.51010	1.2652	4.0992
MOTOPOP	49	0.75301	0.10512	0.50952	0.98039
AREAVEH	49	0.36962E-01	0.49955E-01	0.15079E-02	0.22553
Independent (Political Culture)					
NEWLQ	49	41.035	19.762	3.3333	87.083
PC	49	4.8832	2.6493	0.49746	9.0000
PCSQ	49	30.721	27.631	0.24746	81.000
COMBDEM	49	0.58043	0.19049	0.19231	0.94828
GOVS	49	0.67347	0.47380	0.00000	1.0000
GOVPOW	49	22.000	2.8211	15.000	29.000
FEMTOT	49	0.14391	0.65599E-01	0.22989E-01	0.33019

Table B-7

Sample Statistics on Data Series (1984)

VARIABLE	OBS	MEAN	STD ERROR	MINIMUM	MAXIMUM
Dependent (Adjusted Expenditures)					
CAPEXP	49	2665.0	500.01	2044.0	5124.6
NETGENEX	49	2404.6	486.42	1777.2	4904.2
CAPEXPOP	49	2334.4	379.03	1804.8	3910.8
WELPOOR	49	2332.0	1032.0	1019.3	4540.2
WELPOORN	49	1004.3	598.39	229.16	2402.2
NETHHOS	49	124.03	39.873	70.104	275.68
HHOPCAP	49	226.25	77.250	127.63	458.37
SAFECAP	49	153.53	40.234	88.884	285.79
CORRECAP	49	53.224	20.798	20.424	120.28
NETELED	49	3476.1	811.46	2301.7	7126.8
OPELED	49	3675.3	733.62	2489.3	6339.7
NETHIED	49	4291.3	1472.3	991.87	9540.9
OPHIED	49	8350.6	1510.7	5477.2	13614.
HWTOCAR	49	336.37	108.50	184.11	765.82
HWOPCAR	49	162.81	51.762	77.384	319.56
Independent (Characteristics)					
POVP89A	49	0.13614	0.33798E-01	0.67108E-01	0.23308
METPCT	49	0.63557	0.22236	0.18900	1.0000
ELDPCT	49	0.11778	0.18420E-01	0.77000E-01	0.17600
YNGPCT	49	0.27237	0.25445E-01	0.22900	0.37900
HEATDD	49	4951.1	2126.2	0.00000	9075.0
CRIMRAT9	49	0.45662E-01	0.11982E-01	0.23359E-01	0.68212E-01
MILPVEH	49	0.35148E-01	0.27775E-01	0.63793E-02	0.12481
CAPINCA	49	14.850	1.7096	11.510	18.847
HIEDPCT	49	0.30871E-01	0.61821E-02	0.19667E-01	0.45983E-01
ELSCHPCT	49	0.17113	0.17996E-01	0.13792	0.24030
FEMHPOOR	49	288.13	84.089	162.53	556.03
ELDPOORA	49	0.91584	0.26587	0.48025	1.7435
YNGPOORA	49	2.1030	0.48787	1.3171	3.8446
MOTOPOP	49	0.74489	0.10577	0.48710	1.0058
AREAVEH	49	0.36734E-01	0.48390E-01	0.15905E-02	0.21467
Independent (Political Culture)					
NEWLQ	49	45.834	20.557	1.2500	82.500
PC	49	4.8832	2.6493	0.49746	9.0000
PCSQ	49	30.721	27.631	0.24746	81.000
COMBDEM	49	0.62080	0.18715	0.21154	0.94828
GOVS	49	0.69388	0.46566	0.00000	1.0000
GOVPOW	49	22.000	2.8211	15.000	29.000
FEMTOT	49	0.13188	0.61313E-01	0.28736E-01	0.28538

Table B-8

Sample Statistics on Data Series (1983)

VARIABLE	OBS	MEAN	STD ERROR	MINIMUM	MAXIMUM
Dependent (Adjusted Expenditures)					
CAPEXP	49	2581.1	468.12	1939.5	4843.6
NETGENEX	49	2320.9	455.83	1723.4	4620.3
CAPEXPOP	49	2257.5	358.06	1724.7	3680.5
WELPOOR	49	2269.4	1011.2	1024.9	4455.1
WELPOORN	49	937.57	590.41	90.637	2301.0
NETHHOS	49	121.24	35.718	60.866	245.45
HHOPCAP	49	221.35	75.313	109.92	453.30
SAFECAP	49	150.25	37.959	88.275	274.29
CORRECAP	49	50.741	19.924	17.795	125.75
NETELED	49	3372.9	736.43	2220.9	6573.5
OPELED	49	3556.4	641.48	2501.6	5797.3
NETHIED	49	4059.6	1459.8	1030.1	10033.
OPHIED	49	8064.7	1657.5	5366.8	13328.
HWTOCAR	49	322.41	96.783	175.20	676.18
HWOPCAR	49	160.19	49.381	83.556	288.39
Independent (Characteristics)					
POVP89A	49	0.13398	0.32793E-01	0.71531E-01	0.23191
METPCT	49	0.63102	0.22370	0.18750	0.97850
ELDPCT	49	0.11629	0.18458E-01	0.76500E-01	0.17500
YNGPCT	49	0.27504	0.24118E-01	0.23150	0.37600
HEATDD	49	4951.1	2126.2	0.00000	9075.0
CRIMRAT9	49	0.47234E-01	0.11693E-01	0.24190E-01	0.67811E-01
MILPVEH	49	0.35262E-01	0.27486E-01	0.66071E-02	0.12949
CAPINCA	49	13.941	1.4966	10.887	17.219
HIEDPCT	49	0.31095E-01	0.61593E-02	0.19752E-01	0.44488E-01
ELSCHPCT	49	0.17274	0.16973E-01	0.13927	0.23362
FEMHPOOR	49	286.98	80.606	163.92	538.22
ELDPOORA	49	0.91498	0.25356	0.48599	1.6217
YNGPOORA	49	2.1527	0.47845	1.3367	3.6767
MOTOPOP	49	0.74267	0.10876	0.47734	1.0172
AREAVEH	49	0.36374E-01	0.45986E-01	0.15760E-02	0.19484
Independent (Political Culture)					
NEWLQ	49	46.153	19.189	0.00000	84.583
PC	49	4.8832	2.6493	0.49746	9.0000
PCSQ	49	30.721	27.631	0.24746	81.000
COMBDEM	49	0.62411	0.18625	0.21154	0.94828
GOVS	49	0.67347	0.47380	0.00000	1.0000
GOVPOW	49	22.000	2.8211	15.000	29.000
FEMTOT	49	0.13130	0.62934E-01	0.17241E-01	0.28538

Table B-9
Sample Statistics on Data Series (1982)

VARIABLE	OBS	MEAN	STD ERROR	MINIMUM	MAXIMUM
Dependent (Adjusted Expenditures)					
CAPEXP	49	2515.4	416.84	1919.9	4335.1
NETGENEX	49	2255.8	400.56	1712.6	4121.3
CAPEXPOP	49	2187.1	322.89	1693.8	3216.3
WELPOOR	49	2289.3	1013.1	796.80	4577.3
WELPOORN	49	967.80	557.38	263.10	2265.5
NETHHOS	49	122.10	35.909	76.379	257.54
HHOPCAP	49	210.16	66.681	106.90	433.05
SAFECAP	49	146.08	35.181	79.035	241.41
CORRECAP	49	46.134	19.255	18.858	130.83
NETELED	49	3265.2	639.76	2144.9	5519.2
OPELED	49	3444.7	562.60	2490.5	4722.6
NETHIED	49	4045.1	1423.8	1491.6	9266.0
OPHIED	49	7851.3	1571.5	5213.6	12732.
HWTOCAR	49	321.91	97.778	162.11	627.97
HWOPCAR	49	156.95	48.948	82.049	278.85
Independent (Characteristics)					
POVP89A	49	0.13165	0.31807E-01	0.76059E-01	0.22847
METPCT	49	0.62646	0.22531	0.18600	0.95700
ELDPCT	49	0.11480	0.18546E-01	0.76000E-01	0.17400
YNGPCT	49	0.27771	0.22895E-01	0.23400	0.37300
HEATDD	49	4951.1	2126.2	0.00000	9075.0
CRIMRAT9	49	0.51031E-01	0.13061E-01	0.25112E-01	0.79010E-01
MILPVEH	49	0.36133E-01	0.28068E-01	0.69231E-02	0.13207
CAPINCA	49	13.689	1.5218	10.818	16.582
HIEDPCT	49	0.31257E-01	0.62179E-02	0.19470E-01	0.45497E-01
ELSCHPCT	49	0.17616	0.17309E-01	0.14257	0.23810
FEMHPOOR	49	286.84	77.095	167.10	525.22
ELDPOORA	49	0.91708	0.24816	0.48384	1.5120
YNGPOORA	49	2.2080	0.47199	1.3700	3.5236
MOTOPOP	49	0.73227	0.11072	0.46633	1.0120
AREAVEH	49	0.37375E-01	0.47411E-01	0.15837E-02	0.19399
Independent (Political Culture)					
NEWLQ	49	41.980	22.409	3.7500	87.500
PC	49	4.8832	2.6493	0.49746	9.0000
PCSQ	49	30.721	27.631	0.24746	81.000
COMBDEM	49	0.59946	0.19534	0.23077	0.96429
GOVS	49	0.55102	0.50254	0.00000	1.0000
GOVPOW	49	22.000	2.8211	15.000	29.000
FEMTOT	49	0.11879	0.62533E-01	0.17241E-01	0.29245

Table B-10
Sample Statistics on Data Series (1981)

VARIABLE	OBS	MEAN	STD ERROR	MINIMUM	MAXIMUM
Dependent (Adjusted Expenditures)					
CAPEXP	49	2528.8	345.29	2010.0	3887.0
NETGENEX	49	2251.2	333.89	1791.7	3700.8
CAPEXPOP	49	2159.2	286.55	1664.8	2917.9
WELPOOR	49	2367.1	1004.8	844.86	4719.5
WELPOORN	49	974.73	557.95	-99.875	2338.4
NETHHOS	49	119.50	29.744	74.581	233.56
HHOPCAP	49	202.81	59.996	107.48	368.42
SAFECAP	49	142.09	33.850	80.792	243.26
CORRECAP	49	44.275	17.163	17.206	107.12
NETELED	49	3141.7	558.01	1966.1	4584.7
OPELED	49	3349.4	514.14	2396.0	4334.2
NETHIED	49	4075.5	1294.0	1409.0	7442.9
OPHIED	49	7827.2	1564.4	4952.5	12427.
HWTOCAR	49	349.28	101.21	194.33	631.66
HWOPCAR	49	157.46	45.067	78.524	272.61
Independent (Characteristics)					
POVP89A	49	0.12836	0.30679E-01	0.82357E-01	0.22323
METPCT	49	0.62190	0.22719	0.18450	0.94950
ELDPCT	49	0.11308	0.18486E-01	0.75000E-01	0.17300
YNGPCT	49	0.28190	0.21857E-01	0.23700	0.37100
HEATDD	49	4951.1	2126.2	0.00000	9075.0
CRIMRAT9	49	0.53722E-01	0.13566E-01	0.26187E-01	0.85920E-01
MILPVEH	49	0.36519E-01	0.28655E-01	0.70052E-02	0.13454
CAPINCA	49	13.794	1.4860	11.048	16.464
HIEDPCT	49	0.30970E-01	0.62698E-02	0.19257E-01	0.46295E-01
ELSCHPCT	49	0.17973	0.16268E-01	0.14664	0.23483
FEMHPOOR	49	287.45	71.413	167.27	49,4.46
ELDPOORA	49	0.92414	0.24267	0.48724	1.3842
YNGPOORA	49	2.2960	0.48046	1.4245	3.4235
MOTOPOP	49	0.73267	0.10291	0.46142	0.99388
AREAVEH	49	0.38149E-01	0.49132E-01	0.16579E-02	0.20084
Independent (Political Culture)					
NEWLQ	49	37.722	20.108	1.2500	80.385
PC	49	4.8832	2.6493	0.49746	9.0000
PCSQ	49	30.721	27.631	0.24746	81.000
COMBDEM	49	0.60130	0.19641	0.23077	0.96429
GOVS	49	0.55102	0.50254	0.00000	1.0000
GOVPOW	49	22.000	2.8211	15.000	29.000
FEMTOT	49	0.11761	0.63573E-01	0.11494E-01	0.29245

Table B-11

Sample Statistics on Data Series (1980)

VARIABLE	OBS	MEAN	STD ERROR	MINIMUM	MAXIMUM
Dependent (Adjusted Expenditures)					
CAPEXP	49	2543.4	334.82	1944.4	3712.6
NETGENEX	49	2273.7	319.53	1810.1	3514.2
CAPEXPOP	49	2144.5	277.51	1653.5	2839.2
WELPOOR	49	2326.9	1014.5	725.00	4721.6
WELPOORN	49	1008.3	571.53	268.45	2397.1
NETHHOS	49	121.55	31.401	70.513	230.00
HHOPCAP	49	200.11	58.961	105.02	350.54
SAFECAP	49	140.63	32.992	78.574	234.07
CORRECAP	49	42.784	15.163	17.135	91.919
NETELED	49	3104.6	519.44	1964.8	4487.5
OPELED	49	3284.6	486.07	2366.0	4197.0
NETHIED	49	4229.2	1338.1	1402.6	8548.7
OPHIED	49	7997.3	1622.8	5042.6	12995.
HWTOCAR	49	384.21	121.34	203.45	744.53
HWOPCAR	49	166.28	56.912	81.758	329.13
Independent (Characteristics)					
POVP89A	49	0.12607	0.30213E-01	0.84136E-01	0.22020
METPCT	49	0.61735	0.22933	0.15300	0.94900
CPIDEX	49	0.65697	0.35047E-01	0.60409	0.78319
ELDPCT	49	0.11182	0.18484E-01	0.76000E-01	0.17700
YNGPCT	49	0.28639	0.20969E-01	0.24400	0.37050
HEATDD	49	4951.1	2126.2	0.00000	9075.0
CRIMRAT9	49	0.54754E-01	0.14136E-01	0.25516E-01	0.88540E-01
MILPVEH	49	0.37408E-01	0.29541E-01	0.71404E-02	0.13755
CAPINCA	49	13.831	1.4813	10.909	16.763
HIEDPCT	49	0.30112E-01	0.61282E-02	0.18918E-01	0.46631E-01
ELSCHPCT	49	0.18482	0.14990E-01	0.15293	0.23370
FEMHPOOR	49	287.07	68.989	161.99	469.04
ELDPOORA	49	0.93030	0.24217	0.48814	1.3633
YNGPOORA	49	2.3761	0.49682	1.4736	3.6667
MOTOPOP	49	0.72507	0.98156E-01	0.45531	0.98316
AREAVEH	49	0.39384E-01	0.51568E-01	0.16356E-02	0.21624
Independent (Political Culture)					
NEWLQ	49	42.167	18.406	15.000	77.692
PC	49	4.8832	2.6493	0.49746	9.0000
PCSQ	49	30.721	27.631	0.24746	81.000
COMBDEM	49	0.62919	0.19298	0.29333	0.97143
GOVS	49	0.63265	0.48708	0.00000	1.0000
GOVPOW	49	22.000	2.8211	15.000	29.000
FEMTOT	49	0.97345E-01	0.56412E-01	0.11494E-01	0.26887

Table B-12

Sample Statistics on Data Series (1979)

VARIABLE	OBS	MEAN	STD ERROR	MINIMUM	MAXIMUM
Dependent (Adjusted Expenditures)					
CAPEXP	49	2539.1	324.95	1884.1	3573.8
NETGENEX	49	2270.6	307.90	1715.1	3360.6
CAPEXPOP	49	2156.2	277.75	1640.4	2825.3
WELPOOR	49	2356.0	1024.6	668.56	5166.5
WELPOORN	49	1024.8	541.65	317.80	2189.2
NETHHOS	49	122.53	31.652	75.780	242.44
HHOPCAP	49	196.62	57.725	98.060	353.93
SAFECAP	49	140.95	34.790	78.122	260.36
CORRECAP	49	40.560	12.730	18.154	71.298
NETELED	49	3004.7	494.99	2082.9	4092.2
OPELED	49	3201.5	472.52	2397.6	4157.8
NETHIED	49	4412.6	1231.0	1169.8	7392.5
OPHIED	49	8078.4	1657.9	5134.7	12502.
HWTOCAR	49	373.07	112.18	184.96	716.23
HWOPCAR	49	172.02	56.641	85.459	322.58
Independent (Characteristics)					
POVP89A	49	0.12418	0.30649E-01	0.76504E-01	0.21969
METPCT	49	0.60833	0.22904	0.15300	0.93700
ELDPCT	49	0.11055	0.18575E-01	0.77000E-01	0.18100
YNGPCT	49	0.29088	0.20419E-01	0.25100	0.37000
HEATDD	49	4951.1	2126.2	0.00000	9075.0
CRIMRAT9	49	0.51647E-01	0.14020E-01	0.23253E-01	0.88316E-01
MILPVEH	49	0.37654E-01	0.29183E-01	0.72213E-02	0.14000
CAPINCA	49	14.196	1.5230	11.173	17.375
HIEDPCT	49	0.30066E-01	0.63220E-02	0.18714E-01	0.47705E-01
ELSCHPCT	49	0.19017	0.14162E-01	0.15998	0.23451
FEMHPOOR	49	286.98	67.277	156.42	449.88
ELDPOORA	49	0.93607	0.24544	0.49536	1.4257
YNGPOORA	49	2.4595	0.53886	1.5067	4.0129
MOTOPOP	49	0.72709	0.11949	0.45519	1.1461
AREAVEH	49	0.39525E-01	0.50634E-01	0.16519E-02	0.21402
Independent (Political Culture)					
NEWLQ	49	37.856	18.861	6.8571	76.154
PC	49	4.8832	2.6493	0.49746	9.0000
PCSQ	49	30.721	27.631	0.24746	81.000
COMBDEM	49	0.62980	0.19331	0.29333	0.97143
GOVS	49	0.63265	0.48708	0.00000	1.0000
GOVPOW	49	22.000	2.8211	15.000	29.000
FEMTOT	49	0.97877E-01	0.56313E-01	0.11494E-01	0.26887

Table B-13

Massachusetts Adjusted Annual Expenditures

	1989	1988	1987	1986	1985	1984
CAPEXP	3228.052	3070.239	2971.980	2847.137	2666.172	2571.696
NETGENEX	2909.111	2762.766	2684.797	2545.010	2363.161	2288.433
CAPEXPOP	2894.540	2754.993	2688.495	2585.447	2431.081	2390.788
WELPOOR	5217.567	5089.775	5043.187	5075.594	4631.681	4384.173
WELPOORN	2825.209	2741.147	2895.439	2809.172	2307.904	2151.666
NETHHOS	242.257	213.971	198.839	188.586	175.590	167.310
HHOPCAP	311.589	283.303	268.433	257.910	244.356	237.329
SAFECAP	210.379	202.799	195.450	193.531	187.030	184.906
CORRECAP	77.207	64.624	58.818	55.508	51.450	49.775
NETELED	4397.642	4201.721	4143.379	4027.593	3764.583	3641.838
OPELED	4513.628	4327.093	4353.753	4199.235	3964.301	3914.765
NETHIED	4143.895	4043.816	3890.130	3434.080	4046.460	2898.468
OPHIED	7406.945	7549.584	7359.516	7115.495	6691.900	5878.738
HWTOCAR	255.387	257.972	245.720	222.471	215.056	203.918
HWOPCAR	123.257	123.684	131.116	126.816	125.061	125.798

	1983	1982	1981	1980	1979
CAPEXP	2555.955	2492.258	2614.376	2686.570	2804.246
NETGENEX	2239.892	2174.993	2310.921	2385.712	2480.533
CAPEXPOP	2361.971	2320.665	2420.993	2487.582	2556.341
WELPOOR	4455.139	4577.260	4550.931	4557.752	4380.225
WELPOORN	1940.117	2084.538	2338.398	2397.085	2030.726
NETHHOS	169.273	165.735	169.147	160.281	164.799
HHOPCAP	233.919	225.357	226.418	220.015	207.163
SAFECAP	182.063	174.812	199.507	208.945	212.824
CORRECAP	44.474	42.954	40.513	39.685	38.104
NETELED	3612.316	3458.099	3796.962	3686.307	3934.250
OPELED	3903.190	3795.632	4108.269	3939.837	4157.752
NETHIED	2542.968	2213.322	2038.762	2291.634	2569.687
OPHIED	5628.282	5292.200	4952.470	5216.209	5394.863
HWTOCAR	206.181	206.189	237.351	237.812	248.407
HWOPCAR	122.037	124.807	136.771	141.954	151.418

Table B-14
Massachusetts Demographic and Political Characteristics

	1989	1988	1987	1986	1985	1984
Demographic						
POVP89A	0.107	0.106	0.104	0.102	0.101	0.101
METPCT	0.906	0.906	0.907	0.908	0.909	0.909
ELDPCT	0.137	0.137	0.137	0.136	0.135	0.134
YNGPCT	0.226	0.226	0.228	0.230	0.233	0.235
HEATDD	5593	5593	5593	5593	5593	5593
CRIMRAT9	0.051	0.050	0.047	0.047	0.048	0.046
MILPVEH	0.009	0.009	0.009	0.009	0.009	0.009
CAPINCA	19.379	19.344	18.654	17.902	17.000	16.568
HIEDPCT	0.021	0.021	0.021	0.021	0.021	0.021
ELSCHPCT	0.138	0.141	0.141	0.143	0.145	0.148
FEMHPOOR	430.172	431.063	434.299	435.359	435.866	432.109
ELDPOORA	1.286	1.298	1.323	1.331	1.339	1.331
YNGPOORA	2.122	2.141	2.202	2.251	2.306	2.334
MOTOPOP	0.643	0.650	0.664	0.658	0.642	0.654
AREAVEH	0.002	0.002	0.002	0.002	0.002	0.002
Political						
NEWLQ	89.615	91.154	89.154	85.417	87.083	81.667
PC	3.660	3.660	3.660	3.660	3.660	3.660
PCSQ	13.396	13.396	13.396	13.396	13.396	13.396
COMBDEM	0.800	0.795	0.795	0.790	0.790	0.810
GOVS	1	1	1	1	1	1
GOVPOW	27	27	27	27	27	27
FEMTOT	0.200	0.185	0.185	0.165	0.165	0.130

Table B-14 (continued)					
	1983	1982	1981	1980	1979
Demographic					
POVP89A	0.101	0.100	0.103	0.103	0.105
METPCT	0.895	0.881	0.867	0.853	0.859
ELDPCT	0.132	0.130	0.128	0.126	0.123
YNGPCT	0.240	0.245	0.252	0.258	0.263
HEATDD	5593	5593	5593	5593	5593
CRIMRAT9	0.050	0.055	0.058	0.061	0.059
MILPVEH	0.009	0.009	0.009	0.009	0.009
CAPINCA	15.145	14.362	13.818	13.984	13.909
HIEDPCT	0.022	0.022	0.022	0.021	0.021
ELSCHPCT	0.153	0.157	0.164	0.178	0.181
FEMHPOOR	428.001	421.726	404.362	400.264	387.849
ELDPOORA	1.312	1.297	1.243	1.219	1.176
YNGPOORA	2.386	2.445	2.447	2.501	2.514
MOTOPOP	0.666	0.649	0.651	0.653	0.649
AREAVEH	0.002	0.002	0.002	0.002	0.002
Political					
NEWLQ	84.583	85.000	80.385	77.692	76.154
PC	3.660	3.660	3.660	3.660	3.660
PCSQ	13.396	13.396	13.396	13.396	13.396
COMBDEM	0.810	0.795	0.800	0.815	0.815
GOVS	1	1	1	1	1
GOVPOW	27	27	27	27	27
FEMTOT	0.130	0.095	0.095	0.075	0.075

APPENDIX C

Benchmark Estimating Equations

The following table reports the regression coefficient estimates of the equations used to establish benchmarks in this study.

Table C-1
Benchmark Regression Coefficient Estimates

Coefficient (T-Statistic)	Elementary Education Operating Exps[a]	Higher Education Operating Exps[a]	Net Higher Education Exps[a]	Net Direct Assistance Exps[b]	Net Health & Hospital Exps[c]	Total Highway Exps[d]	Highway Operating Exps[d]	Public Safety Exps[c]	Corrections Exps[c]	Net General Exps[c]
POVP89A	-3660.14 (-2.92)			3518.76 (2.43)	567.36 (6.64)			-33.22 (-0.54)	-54.29 (-1.46)	-126.86 (-0.15)
ELSCHPCT	-12554.02 (-5.94)									-5185.86 (-3.23)
HIEDPCT		-26091.76 (-2.08)	-39571.42 (-3.44)							20547.26 (6.59)
ELDPOORA				607.20 (5.49)						
YNGPOORA				164.10 (2.11)						
FEMHPOOR				1.42 (2.54)						
ELDPCT					-637.20 (-4.96)					-4797.63 (-4.13)
YNGPCT					-311.00 (-2.15)					
MOTOPOP						-443.51 (-10.10)	-208.20 (-10.29)			
MILPVEH						-1724.50 (-5.28)	-411.27 (-2.73)			

[a] Expenditures per student.   [b] Expenditures per poor person.   [c] Expenditures per capita.   [d] Expenditures per vehicle.

	(1)	(2)	(3)	(4)	(5)	(6)	(7)	(8)	(9)	(10)
AREAVEH						1877.05 (9.89)				
HEATDD						0.01 (2.80)	0.01 (3.85)			
CRIMRAT9						912.79 (6.93)	536.82 (6.13)		645.68 (8.09)	
METPCT	-1343.72 (-9.03)	-2915.23 (-7.47)	-1343.59 (-3.76)	360.51 (3.28)	9.33 (0.97)	-252.34 (-9.88)	-142.79 (-12.12)	22.80 (2.56)	-10.02 (-1.85)	-776.23 (-7.75)
CAPINCA	19.13 (0.93)	-67.00 (-1.37)	116.56 (2.60)	70.34 (4.79)	4.13 (2.75)	6.67 (2.45)	1.19 (0.95)	3.48 (3.65)	3.22 (5.55)	48.54 (3.37)
TREND	40.18 (1.29)	78.15 (0.98)	62.91 (0.86)	-12.72 (-0.63)	-5.10 (-2.47)	-12.60 (-3.28)	0.05 (0.03)	5.56 (3.76)	4.43 (4.95)	-4.64 (-0.22)
TRENDSQ	4.24 (1.68)	10.22 (1.55)	-0.86 (-0.14)	1.37 (0.84)	0.51 (3.05)	1.00 (3.15)	-0.10 (-0.98)	-0.24 (-2.08)	-0.13 (-1.80)	4.57 (2.64)
NEWLQ	1.61 (1.01)	0.73 (0.18)	-9.11 (-2.39)	0.56 (0.49)	-0.02 (.00)	-0.54 (-2.59)	-0.16 (-1.63)	-0.33 (-4.58)	-0.09 (-2.09)	-1.37 (-1.27)
PC	221.50 (3.85)	-436.24 (-2.85)	13.73 (0.10)	-80.23 (-2.02)	-15.94 (-4.12)	19.09 (2.45)	-7.79 (-2.17)	15.62 (5.94)	5.07 (3.18)	107.07 (2.76)
PCSQ	-32.40 (-5.21)	27.16 (1.59)	-10.39 (-0.67)	-4.82 (-1.13)	1.47 (3.53)	-3.23 (-3.78)	0.36 (0.92)	-1.85 (-6.40)	-0.43 (-2.44)	-18.12 (-4.30)
COMBDEM	1034.55 (4.64)	-1760.26 (-2.99)	2087.57 (3.87)	829.32 (5.33)	0.02 (0.13)	-8.18 (-0.26)	-21.47 (-1.47)	92.80 (6.40)	22.93 (3.66)	668.31 (4.42)
GOVS	32.83 (0.70)	-78.94 (-0.61)	256.00 (2.14)	85.21 (2.65)	7.36 (2.35)	-3.16 (-0.50)	-0.50 (-0.17)	1.03 (0.47)	-1.41 (-1.05)	22.35 (0.71)
GOVPOW	-2.60 (-0.28)	-107.55 (-4.23)	-33.95 (-1.45)	10.53 (1.62)	0.80 (1.28)	5.30 (4.24)	0.72 (1.25)	-0.40 (-0.90)	-0.36 (-1.34)	16.98 (2.68)
FEMTOT	-29.59 (-0.52)	-1367.57 (-0.92)	-1000.69 (-0.74)	-601.21 (-1.61)	-46.70 (-1.22)	362.47 (4.95)	149.96 (4.44)	65.07 (2.53)	-28.53 (-1.83)	-32.03 (-0.08)
REGNE	5517.72 (8.26)	16107.91 (18.10)	2512.24 (3.08)	-1986.46 (-4.72)	195.44 (2.91)	508.85 (9.34)	373.46 (14.86)	-32.10 (-1.95)	-47.89 (-4.80)	2132.51 (3.83)
REGMA	6328.12 (9.67)	14993.45 (15.78)	3865.05 (4.44)	-2238.57 (-5.35)	215.79 (3.26)	560.58 (10.37)	395.21 (15.85)	-32.11 (-1.78)	-33.94 (-3.10)	2381.05 (4.35)

Table C-1 (continued)

Benchmark Regression Coefficient Estimates

Coefficient (T-Statistic)	Elementary Education Operating Exps[a]	Higher Education Operating Exps[a]	Net Higher Education Exps[a]	Net Direct Assistance Exps[b]	Net Health & Hospital Exps[c]	Total Highway Exps[d]	Highway Operating Exps[d]	Public Safety Exps[c]	Corrections Exps[c]	Net General Exps[c]
REGENC	5671.56 (8.33)	15599.04 (15.92)	4295.43 (4.78)	-1910.24 (-4.57)	177.91 (2.62)	548.13 (9.78)	367.83 (14.23)	-45.62 (-2.66)	-49.30 (-4.75)	2027.56 (3.56)
REGWNC	5769.65 (8.71)	16032.47 (15.98)	4694.24 (5.10)	-2172.49 (-5.21)	175.59 (2.58)	642.46 (10.63)	388.08 (13.92)	-43.59 (-2.51)	-49.00 (-4.65)	2146.63 (3.77)
REGSA	5922.41 (8.52)	16799.32 (15.54)	4600.58 (4.64)	-2347.18 (-5.65)	164.47 (2.43)	651.63 (10.80)	380.27 (13.66)	-52.27 (-2.88)	-38.61 (-3.51)	2226.47 (3.85)
REGESC	5406.56 (7.80)	16354.62 (15.36)	4520.74 (4.63)	-2191.75 (-5.06)	121.73 (1.79)	717.89 (11.81)	397.01 (14.16)	-44.72 (-2.40)	-43.83 (-3.88)	2134.10 (3.70)
REGWSC	5660.09 (7.89)	16479.58 (15.67)	4612.20 (4.78)	-2331.96 (-5.30)	148.38 (2.12)	710.59 (11.82)	399.90 (14.42)	-65.91 (-3.52)	-57.44 (-5.06)	2215.21 (3.74)
REGMT	5949.71 (8.50)	16121.33 (16.95)	5431.89 (6.23)	-2295.68 (-5.49)	171.78 (2.54)	541.64 (10.12)	327.40 (13.27)	-9.19 (-0.53)	-28.77 (-2.74)	2471.47 (4.32)
REGPAC	5624.49 (8.27)	16380.70 (16.57)	5730.99 (6.32)	-2388.17 (-5.75)	164.61 (2.47)	530.56 (9.76)	347.53 (13.86)	-21.05 (-1.17)	-33.89 (-3.11)	2165.15 (3.85)
R^2	.63	.47	.37	.79	.34	.68	.69	.71	.67	.58
Observations	539	539	539	539	539	539	539	539	539	539

[a] Expenditures per student.   [b] Expenditures per poor person.   [c] Expenditures per capita.   [d] Expenditures per vehicle.

ABOUT THE AUTHOR

Herman B. ("Dutch") Leonard is the Baker Professor of Public Sector Financial Management at the John F. Kennedy School of Government at Harvard University, where he teaches courses on state and local government finances, tax policy, financial management, management strategy, and leadership. He is a member of numerous national panels and task forces, including the Research and Education Advisory Panel of the United States General Accounting Office and the Task Force on Infrastructure Reporting of the Governmental Accounting Standards Board. He is currently a member of the Board of Directors of the Massachusetts Health and Educational Facilities Authority. During the 1980s, he chaired the Massachusetts Governor's Task Force on College Opportunity and was a member of the Governor's Advisory Council on Infrastructure, the National Academy of Sciences Committee on National Urban Policy, the U.S. Senate Budget Committee Private Sector Advisory Council on Infrastructure Financing, and the Alaska Governor's Council on Economic Policy.

Professor Leonard has written and published extensively on public finance issues. His 1986 book, *Checks Unbalanced,* focuses on the hidden costs of off-budget government spending. His research has concentrated on issues of public sector financial accountability.

Professor Leonard received his AB, AM, and PhD degrees in economics from Harvard University, concentrating in econometrics and public finance. He was a Junior Fellow in the Harvard University Society of Fellows from 1976 to 1979, when he joined the faculty of the Kennedy School. He lives in Concord, Massachusetts, with his wife Kathryn Angell and daughters Whitney and Dana.

PIONEER PUBLICATIONS

In Print:

Pioneer Paper No. 1, *The Massachusetts Health Plan: The Right Prescription?* by Attiat F. Ott and Wayne B. Gray, Clark University, published 1988.

Pioneer Paper No. 2, *The Cost of Regulated Pricing: A Critical Analysis of Auto Insurance Premium Rate-Setting in Massachusetts* by Simon Rottenberg, University of Massachusetts at Amherst, published 1989.

Pioneer Paper No. 3, *Work and Welfare in Massachusetts: An Evaluation of the ET Program* by June O'Neill, Baruch College, published 1990.

Pioneer Paper No. 4, *Mental Retardation Programs: How Does Massachusetts Compare?* by Edward Moscovitch, Cape Ann Economics, published 1991.

Pioneer Paper No. 5, *School Choice in Massachusetts* by Abigail Thernstrom, published 1991.

Pioneer Dialogue No. 1, *Thoughts on School Reform,* the proceedings of a Pioneer luncheon forum and two symposiums held at Harvard University, published 1989.

Pioneer Dialogue No. 2, *Bay State Auto Rates: What Are the Driving Forces?,* the proceedings of a Pioneer luncheon forum, published 1990.

Pioneer Compendium No. 1, *Invitation to Change,* edited by Jeremiah Cole and Virginia Straus, Better Government Competition, 1991 Winners.

Forthcoming:

Steven F. Wilson, Pioneer co-director, on the Boston school system.